THE HEART
OF SINGING

STEPS ON THE PATH TO BECOMING
THE SINGER YOU WANT TO BE

To Jim —

Joyful Singing !

Diane

DIANE HASLAM

ISBN: 1453696067
ISBN-13: 9781453696064
LCCN: 2010910217

"Everyone Sang", from *Collected Poems of Siegfried Sassoon,* © 1918 and 1920 by E.P. Dutton, © 1936, 1946, 1947, 1948 by Siegfried Sassoon, reprinted by kind permission of the Estate of George Sassoon and Viking Penguin, a division of Penguin Group (USA) Inc..

"Piano" and "Escape" by D.H.Lawrence reproduced by kind permission of Pollinger Limited and The Estate of Frieda Lawrence Ravagli.

Excerpt from "What Do the Simple Folk Do?" from *Camelot* by Alan Jay Lerner and Frederick Loewe, ©1960 (Renewed) Alan Jay Lerner and Frederick Loewe Publication and Allied Rights assigned to Chappell and Co., Inc., reprinted by kind permission of Alfred Music Publishing.

Excerpt from *A Return to Love: Reflections on the Principles of a Course in Miracles* by Marianne Williamson, © 1992 by Marianne Williamson, reprinted by kind permission of the author.

Excerpt from "The Earth Worm Also Sings" from *Roots of the Moment* by Pauline Oliveros, © 1998 by Pauline Oliveros, reprinted by kind permission of the author and the Deep Listening Institute, Ltd.

Quotation from *Flow: The Psychology of Optimal Experience* by Mihaly Csikszentmihaly, © 1990 by Mihaly Csikszentmihaly, used by kind permission of the author.

Quotation from *The Art of Possibility* by Rosamund Stone Zander and Benjamin Zander, © 2000 by Rosamund Zander and Benjamin Zander, used by kind permission of the authors.

Quotations from *The Right to Speak* by Patsy Rodenburg, © 1992 by Patsy Rodenburg, used by kind permission of the author.

Quotation from *Thomas Merton: Spiritual Master, The Essential Writings; edited with an Introduction by Lawrence S. Cunningham,* copyright ©1992 by Lawrence S. Cunningham, reprinted by kind permission of Paulist Press, Inc. www.paulistpress.com, and the Merton Legacy Trust.

Quotation from *Singing and Imagination: A Human Approach to a Great Musical Tradition* by Thomas Hemsley, © 1998 by Thomas Hemsley, used by kind permission of Oxford University Press and the author.

www.dianehaslam.com

*Dedicated to my husband, Bruce, and
my mother, Sheila*

Contents

ACKNOWLEDGEMENTS

WITH GRATEFUL THANKS...

To my husband, Bruce Hammond, for his unfailing love, patience, and support; to my mother, Sheila Haslam, without whose active and invaluable help and encouragement I could never have finished this project; to my father, Ivan Haslam, for all I learned from him that has kept me grounded through the process; to Karen Zagrodnik, for her generosity and help with initial editing; to Janet Wagner, for her excellent editing and advice; to my great friends, Eve Konstantine, for her belief in me all these years, Blythe Walker, for sharing her wisdom about the art form she loves, and Annasue McCleave Wilson, for providing a race to the finish! Also, to all of the teachers in my life, particularly Pamela Cook, the voice teacher who launched me on my singing path, and to all my dear students, past and present, who have taught me so much.

Author's Note

Some readers will find everything in this book new and thought provoking. Some will recognize parts of it from their previous experience. Some will be very familiar with many of the concepts but surprised by a few new ideas. Some may think they've heard it all already. It is deliberately written with a broad brushstroke, but whatever your experience so far, I believe there will be value, if not revelations, for you somewhere in this book. If there are sections that some more knowledgeable readers find overly familiar, it is fine to skip forward. But don't underestimate the value of visiting familiar places afresh, looking with new eyes, or simply reminding yourself of certain ideas.

I have deliberately avoided using too much "singer talk"—language familiar to many teachers and voice students from their "vocal pedagogy" classes but which can alienate the general reader.

For simplicity's sake, I have alternated the pronouns *he* and *she* when referring to the singer or the teacher or the listener.

INTRODUCTION

"If one really wishes to be master of an art, technical knowledge of it is not enough. One has to transcend technique so that the art becomes an 'artless art' growing out of the Unconscious."
– Daisetz T. Suzuki,
from the introduction to Zen in the Art of Archery

"We are all on a journey; we are all at different stages of our journey, but what's certain is: none of us has yet arrived."
– Rev. Steven van Kuiken

Singing is a journey. While traveling this road, we have the possibility of personal growth, deeper insights, and magical experiences. There is always somewhere interesting to go, new paths to explore, and adventures to be had. Not even the greatest of singers (especially not the greatest of singers!) would say they have "arrived." What great singers understand is that there is far too much joy to be experienced in the changes and growth to stay put for long. But learning to sing is a bumpy and difficult path filled with numerous potholes to trip us up and roadblocks to deter us from our route, threatening to halt our progress. Negotiating the physical and mental demands of our journey can be exhausting and discouraging. Staying where we are often seems simpler and always easier, no matter whether we are experienced professionals or beginners. What I hope to give you with this book is:

- Insight into the joys and rewards of singing.
- Reasons to keep on growing through development of your voice.
- Understanding of your role on this journey.
- Thoughts about how to make your journey easier.
- Encouragement to stay on your path, wherever you might be right now.

This is not a "how-to-sing" manual. If you need help under-standing the physiology of singing or have specific technical problems, find a voice teacher. *There is no substitute for a good voice teacher.* Singers all need someone objective to listen and guide, to watch and encourage. A book cannot do that. But, all too often, voice teachers are expected to be gurus, or, if not quite that, at least to be able to fix all our problems if we give them a few hours of our time and a generous donation from our bank account. If we follow what they say to the letter, we believe we will solve all our vocal problems, be successful, and become a star. We think that learning to sing is like learning to drive or to swim, and there is a magical formula that we just have to master to be able to sing the way we imagine we can and that once we've learned it, we'll never forget.

Why is it that this works for so few singers? Because voice les-sons are only part of the story.

Most voice teachers will guide us through the maze of vocal technique: teaching us about the vocal tract, laryngeal positions, glottal closure, and velar elevation; explaining the musculature of the vocal mechanism; defining *appoggio, copertura,* and *tessitura.* From our voice teacher we may hear about placement, reso-nance, articulation, and phonation. Our teacher will most likely spend a lot of time focusing on specific problems, dissecting what is going wrong and concentrating on how to fix things. This leads to a strong emphasis on left-brain function—analysis, atten-tion to detail, and intellectual (versus intuitive) understanding. This is a necessary part of learning to sing, and I want to stress its importance, but that is exactly what it is—a part. The vital balance of the right-brain function—the creativity, the intuition, and the broader view—is just as, if not more, important, but it is extremely difficult to address in the private voice studio. It is a side of learning to sing for which you, the singer, are entirely, solely responsible.

In my view, the very foundations of great singing are not learned in the studio; we teach them to ourselves through greater self-knowledge. Through this book I want to lead you to the great teacher inside of you and help you hear its voice. I hope to give you the courage to believe in your potential and strengthen the positive aspects of yourself and your voice. Together we will take a holistic look at singing, remembering that nothing is separate, and find the path to the connections between the parts. If you imagine singing as a tree, this will remind you of the importance of the deep roots and strong trunk that allow the branches and leaves a chance to grow. It will guide you to your authentic self, the part of you that can lead you to a clearer, purer, freer voice— the one you lost so many years ago or maybe the one you have been seeking all along.

My Journey

I have been singing for as long as I can remember. My mother was my role model, and my memories of her are filled with the sound of her beautiful voice. She would sing all the time—around the house, in the car, and even as we shopped in the market together. She took leads in local musical theater productions and sang with big bands and in clubs. In my eyes my mother was a glamorous star, and I wanted to be like her.

At the age of about eight, I sang my first solo in public—a verse from "All Things Bright and Beautiful" at church. From that moment, I wanted nothing else but to sing. I nagged my parents for voice lessons, and when I was twelve, they finally gave in and sent me to a wonderful teacher, Pamela Cook. My teenage years were filled with only positive musical experiences, mostly created by my participation in a girls' choir called Cantamus, which my voice teacher founded from a group of her own young students. We performed on television and in concerts all over Britain, and we traveled the world winning competitions. Our director challenged us to memorize extremely complex choral music that ranged from Renaissance motets to contemporary classical works and we mastered songs in numerous languages— no small feat for girls from a small, blue-collar community. I became addicted to the emotional ride the music took me on and knew I could never consider any other path. Singing had already become a vital part of my life.

My experience in college was not such a positive one. Because I was so set on my path, I went straight from high school to a conservatory at the age of eighteen—in hindsight I realize it was too early in my vocal development for me to fully benefit from what college had to offer. The focus at my college was on training classical singers in opera, and I found myself singing alongside singers with much bigger voices than mine. It was there I discovered that size matters! I wasn't going to get anywhere in the opera productions unless my voice became bigger and stronger. Although I had a very good voice teacher, my lack of maturity wasn't allowing me to hear most of the wisdom she had to impart; all I wanted was to sound like my heroes and sing louder because I thought I would then be cast in the operas. I had always been a good actor and loved being on stage, and my emotional commitment and development were way ahead of most. But my voice wasn't. So I tried to make it catch up quickly and in the process, unknowingly created bad habits it would take me years to recognize, let alone undo.

This didn't mean I was deterred from my path, and by sheer will power I was able to manage my imperfect voice well enough to make a full-time living as a singer for many years. I wasn't a star, but I was happy to accept that fact if I could just keep singing. I kept working on my voice with different voice teachers, but no one seemed to have the magic formula to undo the vocal knots I had tied. Then I began to realize an important truth: it wasn't only *vocal* knots I was dealing with—I had *mental* knots too. They manifested themselves in various ways. Whenever I had a solo performance coming up, I would get sick in some way: sometimes a cold, sometimes a sore throat, sometimes a cough, and occasionally complete laryngitis. The pattern became obvious: I was sabotaging myself. Usually I would still get through the performance but never to my satisfaction because I couldn't perform optimally. I was also always looking outside myself for excuses. For example, my first husband was a brilliant musician with very high standards and few encouraging words, so my mission became to please him. When I didn't seem to succeed, I blamed him for my lack of success: "If only he would help me or give me encouragement or show more interest." By blaming my health or someone else for my failure, I was relinquishing responsibility for my own performance.

As soon as I identified this, my path changed drastically. I began to change my attitude to my problems and take control of my voice. I came to realize that what I was thinking had the greatest influence on how I performed, not what was happening on the outside. When I began teaching singing, I learned more about the habits, both physical and mental, that singers so easily fall into. I began to see in my students a reflection of my own bad habits and I slowly learned to let go and move toward a freer voice, one that I could use to the full to experience the joys of singing and express my whole spirit.

My journey has not been easy, nor is it over. I learn about my voice every day. No day is exactly the same, and nothing is entirely predictable. Today I am different from yesterday, and tomorrow I will again be changed—and my voice along with me. Accepting that is part of the great joy and the great lesson of this singing journey.

Through my teaching, I have discovered that the singer's journey is a common path. I have observed many different students of all ages, levels, and types. I have taught them to sing the full gamut of styles ranging from opera to musical theater, pop to rock, classical to jazz, and beyond. At our roots, we share so much—hopes, fears, dreams, and needs—and singing allows us to express these common themes, as well as experience and address them. In all cases I have discovered that at its heart success in singing is about our ability first to discover our own true voice—our *authentic voice*—and then to be prepared to share ourselves through our singing.

YOUR TALENT

According to popular belief, talent is something you are born with. Musical talent, acting talent, athletic talent, mathematical talent, or whatever it might be—you either have it or you don't. First comes the talent, and then the lessons to develop, hone, and perfect it.

I want to help you see that the talent of a singer is, perhaps more than in any other field, WHO YOU ARE. It is not about your voice but your *honesty*, not about how beautiful your tone is but about your *commitment*, and not about your sound but about your *authenticity*. At the heart of every great singer are qualities that provide the foundation for application of the technique that is learned and which becomes the basis for success. You have every possibility of becoming the great singer you want to be, if you can only strengthen this core, grow into your true self, and find your free voice. It is there inside everyone—even inside those who have never believed themselves to be singers. If you have ever said "I'd love to be able to sing," then you have the potential to be thoroughly successful as a singer.

I will add one word of caution: this journey takes courage. Fear, in its many different and varied manifestations, is the root of so many of our problems in singing that I will address it in some way in almost every chapter of this book. So whether you are embarking on this journey or continuing it, you must always be prepared to face your fears. There is no total escape from them, but there are ways of minimizing them, weakening their power, and making them easier to live with. I hope to help you with that, too.

WHERE THE PATH LEADS

First and foremost this book is for any singer who truly wants to reach his full potential, who wants to be the best he can be, and who is prepared to do the work to get there. But always bear in mind that "none of us has yet arrived." We are not on our singing journey in order to reach a final destination. We may reach certain goals and attain a certain level of achievement and satisfaction, but there is always somewhere else to go, another path to take. That is what makes singing so exciting and so enticing. You may begin with one goal in mind, but as you travel, your experiences transform it, and you find yourself on an entirely new path. Goals are only resting places, where you take stock for a while and move on to your next fascinating encounter. With this book I hope to help you experience not only the thrill of this singing journey but also the joy of being exactly *where you are.*

Thoreau once said, in reference to walking in the woods "the thought of some work will run in my head and I am not where my body is—I am out of my senses. What business have I in the woods, if I am thinking of something out of the woods?" By being right in the present moment, experiencing your voice fully, faults and all, here and now, actually creates for you the momentum to move forward and learn to develop your full potential. With each chapter I will show you how to more fully experience your voice with honesty, trust, and confidence. I will lead you to the understanding that the voice of the singer you've always wanted to be is *the voice of the singer you already are:* it simply needs encouragement and guidance to reveal itself.

THE FOUNDATIONS

I have said that I am not going to teach about specific vocal technique as such, though some of the topics and exercises may well prove useful technically. My initial aim with this book is to pass on some thoughts and suggestions about what I see as the *fundamentals* of singing, the foundation stones on which everything is built, and which will establish the grounding for success and the revelation of the singer you know yourself to be. With these foundations strengthened, the technique you learn becomes easier to apply, your path to success smoother, and your sense of fulfillment enhanced.

I will explain how you must:

- **Acknowledge the Power:** Understand the importance singing has in the world, recognize the value of singing, and clarify your own reasons for singing.
- **Embark on the Path to Self-Discovery:** Find your fearless core, acknowledge your Authentic Singer, and confront the Diva.
- **Understand Commitment:** Learn about full commitment and how to experience it, and then discover what you need to commit to in practice and performance.
- **Take Control of Your Thoughts:** Recognize the chattering voices in your head, understand the role of the left and right brain, use meditation to improve your singing, get into *flow,* and transform your fears.

- **Eliminate the Judge:** Learn how to silence the Inner Judge, deal with other Judges, drop comparisons, and discover your best.
- **Trust Your Breath:** Understand the importance of breath, learn about its power, and realize its connection to the whole.
- **Tend to Your Body:** Learn to use the whole body to sing, find your physical weak spots, understand the importance of center core strength and grounding, and pinpoint the source of your singing energy.
- **Open Up to Creativity, Flexibility, and Growth:** Expand your vocal possibilities, learn creative listening, "feel" your voice, open yourself to new sounds and sensations, and expand the imagination.
- **Find Balance:** Understand the importance of balance, avoid extremes, find emotional balance, and learn how to give and take with an audience.

Following these steps will not necessarily guarantee fame and fortune—the essence of which has also much to do with elements of character, drive, marketing, and serendipity, which are beyond the realm of this book. But working on these principles, reminding yourself of them regularly, and using them as a basis for all your singing experiences will help you to achieve the satisfaction you want from your singing life.

They are the steps on the path to becoming the singer you want to be.

CHAPTER 1

POWER PLAY

ACKNOWLEDGING THE POWER OF SINGING

Everyone suddenly burst out singing;
And I was filled with such delight
As prisoned birds must find in freedom
Winging wildly across the white
Orchards and dark green fields; on - on - and out of sight.

Everyone's voice was suddenly lifted;
And beauty came like the setting sun:
My heart was shaken with tears, and horror
Drifted away...O, but Everyone
Was a bird; and the song was wordless; the singing
will never be done.
– Siegfried Sassoon, *"Everyone Sang"*

Written in 1918, at the end of World War I, Sassoon's poem reminds me of the true story of a Christmas Eve on the Western Front in the Great War, when one German soldier began to sing "Stille Nacht" ["Silent Night"] from his position on one side of No Man's Land. Soon, not only the German troops but also the British in the opposite trenches joined in, until they were all singing a medley of Christmas carols. This spontaneous outburst led to these soldiers of opposing camps emerging from their respective dugouts to share cigarettes, food, stories, play soccer together, and sing more songs, just for a few hours until daybreak. Singing, for a short time at least, was the catalyst for peace between bitter enemies. Perhaps it was this very moment that inspired Sassoon's poem.

Throughout history we see evidence of the importance of song. The singing of spirituals helped give African slaves the strength, courage, and sense of companionship to do their back-breaking work; sea shanties were sung in rhythm to help sailors work together to haul the rigging or raise the anchor; in the eighteenth and nineteenth centuries, Scottish women sang "waulking songs" while they performed the tedious work of softening heavy tweed cloth by rubbing or banging it against a board; coal miners the world over improvised songs together to take their minds off the hellish work conditions in the mines; and hymns and gospel songs have transformed the lives of people the world over by inspiring hope and faith.

Perhaps the most significant examples of the power of singing come from places where it is used either as a tool for peace or a weapon in the struggle against oppression. The songs of the black South African musicians in the 1960s gave voice to the sufferings of the blacks and played a huge part in motivating the revolution that led to the end of apartheid[1]. More recently, in the war-torn African nation of Angola, a project was initiated by the Washington-based nongovernmental organization (NGO) Search for Common Ground called *Music for Peace*. Twenty-four musicians from all parts of the country made a recording; musicians from opposing sides of the conflict who would not normally be heard performing together were now singing in harmony and promoting peace and partnership across ethnic and political divides. It was released to coincide with upcoming elections. The aim of the CD was explained by SFCG as "an effort to reach out to Angolan youth through music, in order to catalyze a shift toward a new Angolan attitude that celebrates cooperation, participation, and hope in the future." The title track is "Angola, Solta a Tua Voz" [Angola, Lift up your Voice].

Another story of the power of song comes from the small Baltic nation of Estonia. For 150 years, the country has held a massive Song Festival in a special park in Tallinn where 20,000 singers join voices to sing as one. It has always been a very special event. During the twentieth century the country suffered first under the oppression of the Russians, then, during World War II,

---

[1]   The film *Amandla: A Revolution in Four-Part Harmony* so beautifully and powerfully documents this time in South African history.

of the Nazis, and were reoccupied by the Russians in 1944. Great hardship, abuse, and deprivation resulted from the occupation. A resistance movement began in 1988 that was aptly named the Singing Revolution because it included mass gatherings at the Song Festival grounds, where night singing demonstrations were held. At the first meeting 300,000 people—one third of the population of the country—gathered to sing songs that were forbidden by the Russian occupation. The folk songs of the country became songs of freedom that kept the hopes and courage of the people alive and unified the ethnic Estonians. The result was a totally peaceful revolution that led to the country gaining independence in 1991[2].

Closer to home, it isn't hard to see the significance of singing in our own lives. Simply take a look at any important rituals like weddings, worship services, graduation ceremonies, wakes, birthdays, or celebrations of all sorts, and you will see singing and songs taking center stage as an essential ingredient. But the power of singing does not only manifest itself on momentous occasions or in world-shattering ways. Singing in all its forms can be healing, liberating, cathartic, revelatory, or mood changing for both listener and singer. I passionately believe that singing has both mental and physical benefits, and, from the number of people around the world who want to sing (it's up there at the top of many a wish list!), it seems the world agrees. If we're open and willing to look, singing can uncover things we never knew about ourselves. Whether we're bursting out in song in the shower or performing at Carnegie Hall or listening to our favorite singer on the radio, singing has intrinsic restorative and soul-uplifting possibilities.

Why is this? There are several reasons that are worth considering. In contrast to instrumental music, singing has in its favor (at least, most commonly) the added dimension of words. These allow people to more directly trigger personal associations and memories. But it is only partly the communion of words and music that gives songs their power. Even if there are no words, as in the case of a mother simply humming a soft melody to her child or the scatting of a wonderful jazz singer, the power of singing is still evident.

---

2   *The Singing Revolution* is a documentary film by James and Maureen Tusty about these events in the history of Estonia.

THE ROOTS OF THE POWER

Let us look at the process of singing and its effect on us. For the singer herself, it begins with the movement of breath into the body, a deep inhalation whose energy is taken under control by the abdominal and diaphragmatic muscles. The exhalation is instilled with the energy of the emotion conveyed by the particular song, and the quality of the airflow is determined by that emotion. On its way out of the body, the pressure of the air initiates vibrations of the vocal folds, and the breath energy is transformed into sound waves. The sound created is propelled into the resonance cavities in the head, throat, and chest where more vibrations are set up. These are then transferred into the surrounding space and sent toward the listener, shaped by vowel formations and punctuated by consonants as necessary. This physical experience of singing is transmitted to the listener both by the shared experience of the vibrations and the sense of exertion it took to make them happen. As the singer sings, the listener is *virtually* singing: just as when you watch a love scene or a fistfight in a movie, your body may respond as if only once removed from the action, so the listener *feels* the singing. This can only happen because the experience of singing is universal, unlike other musical experiences such as playing the violin.

When we sing, then, we are essentially communicating through our life source, our breath, which is transformed into sound waves. The vibrations occurring both in the singer's body and in the listener's ears set up a direct and powerful connection between people. Perhaps our taste in singers is all to do with which singer has not only words and melodies we relate to but also those vibrations that synchronize with vibrations in our own body.

THE POWER OF SINGING TOGETHER

When people sing *together*, they become both the generators and receivers of the sound vibrations and strong bonds of connection can be created that imply unanimity. Maybe it was this sense of unity implied in the perfect harmony of the songs of the blacks in pre-revolution South Africa that instilled fear in the white minority dictators, as well as providing a comfort and support for the singers themselves. In such a context, the power of singing becomes clear.

So, if there is any group activity that exemplifies the adage "The whole is greater than the sum of its parts", a choir is it. The attraction it holds for many people is that as part of the choir, they have the power to create something great that far exceeds anything they could ever accomplish individually. Along with the possibility of transformation of what one may see as minimal talent into amazing power, belonging to a singing group also enhances teamwork, calls for cooperation, refines discipline, and above all—the key here —*submerges the individual ego*. Put an extrovert, a painfully shy person, a billionaire, and a welfare recipient together in a choir, and they cease to fit those definitions as they work together to create something beautiful, spiritual, and satisfying while having fun in the process! What great joy can be experienced both in rehearsal and in performance, and the effect on others can often be profound.

I am music director of a community choir in South Carolina. No audition is required to participate in the choir, you don't have to be able to read music, and you don't even have to have any singing skills. You just have to want to be part of the choir and enjoy singing together. This presents many challenges for me musically but I would have it no other way. For some of the singers, this is their only opportunity to sing, and the joy this choir brings to them is reward enough for the effort. And when we take our popular songs of the 30s and 40s into nursing homes and retirement communities, the power of singing is manifestly evident; we do not have to achieve perfection to illicit tears of joy and gratitude from our audience for bringing back memories with familiar tunes and giving them the sense of still being cared for and thought about by the world "outside."

Sing in a choir and you will experience the power of singing.

The Empathy of Singing

I believe another reason for the universal power of singing is that songs often feel like an expression of empathy to the listener.

Empathy is recognized as being a vital tool in relationships and in the creation of bonds between people. It is used as a solution to conflict in domestic or global confrontations. If one party feels empathy from another, a sense of fellowship and understanding is created and certain fears or feelings of isolation are quelled.

Through songs, the singer stirs reminders of past feelings in the audience and in effect says "I've felt what you felt—I understand." The listener recognizes the common experience and feels comforted to hear someone expressing what he himself has known. Out of the mouth of the singer comes the reflection of the listener's own emotions or experience, expressed by someone *who obviously understands and shares that experience.* The listener's response is "I've been in that situation...I've had those feelings...I am not alone...That is my dream too." In this way singing acts to unite us, to help us feel connected to each other, and to help us be part of a common experience. We feel safe.

It seems to me that art of all kinds has this possibility. We look at a painting or hear a symphony performed or read a poem and feel connected to the creator by this sense of a common understanding. But singing has the added dimension of being a direct and intimate experience. The listener feels the singer is speaking directly to him when the feelings expressed are so familiar. Of course those feelings may be universally shared, even as the experience for the listener is very personal.

Perhaps the most powerful aspect of singing, then, and the reason we find it playing a dominant role in so many cultures, is that singing can reach out and connect us all by expressing our shared experiences.

PERSONAL POWER

"By touching off our vocal power we begin to sense and release all sorts of other power."
– Patsy Rodenburg, *The Right to Speak*

Patsy Rodenburg is a voice coach for many well-known actors and has written extensively on the subject of the voice and how to use it to greatest effect. In her book *The Right to Speak,* she recognizes the power of the human voice in all its manifestations, in speech, as well as in singing. She contends that whether we are singers or actors or simply speakers, if we begin to recognize the power not only of *what* we say but *how* we say (or sing) it, we will discover and sense a multitude of other strengths and possibilities within ourselves. By finding strength through our voice, we can discover a confidence that leads to the manifestation of power in other aspects of our lives. Thus singing becomes a means by which we release our own personal power.

After all, if we dare to sing, don't we dare almost anything?

A beautiful voice that communicates clearly and emotionally can elicit surprising reactions from others. When we use our singing (or speaking) voices with confidence, people are likely to view us as strong or fearless or at the very least special in some way. I have a friend who is particularly short in stature and who had tremendous difficulty getting girlfriends when he was young. He grew to have one of the most beautiful and expressive tenor voices I have ever heard, and now, as a successful operatic tenor, he is, to say the least, very popular! Susan Boyle, the Scottish woman who had kept herself hidden and had never been noticed by anyone, gained the attention of the whole world when she was thrown into the limelight by her unexpectedly riveting performance on the TV show *Britain's Got Talent.* Suddenly she had all sorts of power thrust on her that she had never envisioned.

As singing changes the way others respond to us, a chain of positive shifts may be set up that enhance our lives. If we sense the power we have over others and their response is what we desire, we gain confidence, which leads to our singing with more commitment, and so the cycle of success and improvement begins.

My college students recently were required to perform in a recital of songs, all of which had to be humorous in some way. The first reaction from most of them was to roll their eyes in exasperation, imagining, no doubt, the silly pieces they might be asked to sing and their impending embarrassment in front of their peers. In rehearsals, as the performance loomed, there were numerous presentations of funny songs that fell completely flat because of the half-hearted, fearful performances of self-conscious youngsters. Then, one day shortly before the concert was to take place, things fell into place for one of the students, and the listening group of singers was left rolling in the aisles with laughter at her song—this was the first time she had sung the words clearly enough for them to understand the joke! All of a sudden the bar was set: it became the goal of every other student to elicit the same response from the audience. They recognized that by offering the audience the humor of the song, they had the power to gain the approval they craved. When it came to the night of the show, the energy level was sky high, and every last student sang his piece better than he had ever sung it. The audience went home very happy indeed.

Laughter is a very tangible emotional response which can easily feed a performer. My students discovered through this experience that when you sing with the intention of using the power of your singing to affect someone's emotional state, you are likely to sing better. It gave them a glimpse of what it takes to be successful as a singer.

So it is important to understand that there is not only power *in* singing through the message of the songs we sing, but we also gain personal power *through* the act of singing itself. When we understand this power of singing, we go some way to giving our voices value and worth. In doing so, we can change our motivation and create for ourselves a reason to sing that enhances, rather than diminishes, our own self-image. Instead of allowing singing to fill us with fear, we discover it can give us courage.

THE HEALING POWER

Once, upon the road, I came upon a lad
Singing in a voice three times his size,
When I asked him why, he told me he was sad
And singing always made his spirits rise;
And that's what simple folk do
I surmise.
　　— Alan Jay Lerner and Frederick Loewe,
　　　from "What Do the Simple Folks Do?" from Camelot

It's not just the simple folk—most people have felt the way singing can lift the spirits at some time. We may change our own mood by feeling the pleasant vibrations in our bodies or be transported by the sound of someone else's voice. My dear husband, no trained singer, has discovered the mood-altering power of singing: he only has to sing any simple ditty to me in his pleasant baritone and I'm putty in his hands, a quarrel forgotten or a problem appeased. But there is more to the voice's healing power.

Much detailed research has been done into the capacity of different types of music and singing in particular to cure ills. Books like *The Roar of Silence* by Don Campbell[3], *Toning: The Creative Power of the Voice* by Laurel Elizabeth Keyes, and *Using Voice and Movement in Therapy* by Paul Newham detail the power our own voice has to heal physical and mental problems. A recent study done at George Washington University took a group of 300 elderly people in three cities, half of whom participated for a year in a regular singing group and half of whom did not. The results showed that the group who had been singing experienced fewer falls, illnesses, and bouts of depression; were less likely to complain of loneliness; and had higher self-esteem. Another paper published by Gunter Kreutz, professor of systematic musicology at the Carl von Ossietzky University Oldenburg, concluded that after an hour of choral singing practice, an immune marker in saliva called S-IgA showed marked increase, and the participants registered a happier mood. The results, he concludes, "suggest that choir singing positively influences both emotional affect and immune competence." In other words, the participants were healthier and happier after singing! The conclusions of such research cannot be lightly dismissed.

Like the boy in the song from *Camelot*, it is easy to see how singing could be used to help patients with depression. But in his book *Chanting: Discovering Spirit in Sound*, Robert Gass makes even greater claims. He relates stories of repeated experiments in clinics around the world, where singing has been used as therapy for diseases including cancer. He describes one study conducted in Paris that showed that women with breast cancer who chanted

---

3   Author also of *The Mozart Effect*.

or sang for several hours each day for a month could significantly reduce or even eliminate their tumors. The conclusion was that singing had measurably boosted the immune systems of cancer patients. Gass goes on to explain that singing is so powerful because of its inseparable connection to our physical bodies and our emotional core (unlike an instrument such as a piano that is detached from us). So how we use our voice and how it sounds is bound to affect us physically, mentally, and emotionally.

THE MAGIC OF SINGING

So when we combine the different aspects of singing's power—stimulating physical vibrations, creating a sense of unity, expressing empathy, stirring memory, and healing—it becomes endowed with a certain sense of *magic*. The magician singer can conjure up emotions and change people's lives in a very short amount of time. You can probably think of a time when you have cried at a particular performance or found your bad mood after a tiring day transformed by hearing a favorite song. Every audience is waiting for magic to happen.

As a performer, the singer must first be aware of the magic he can create and then take responsibility for the power of that magic. He must cast the spell as soon as he walks on stage and be careful not to break the spell the moment the song is over. The listener needs time to soak in the magic and experience the feelings that have been stirred.

I often see my students deny the power of their performance by disengaging themselves from the magic before and after they sing. I have one student who has a potentially world-class voice, and her performances can be captivating in their expressiveness. But she spoils the whole thing for her audience by making light of any introduction to her song or playing the clown as she walks on stage, and then giggling at herself or making a joke when she is finished. She pretends not to take her singing seriously.

Her problem is she fears the magic she has created and the responsibility it brings with it. The role of magician is not easy.

FEARING THE POWER

Consider this excerpt from a beautiful poem from *A Return to Love: Reflections on the Principles of a Course in Miracles* by Marianne Williamson:

> *Our deepest fear is not that we are inadequate;*
> *Our deepest fear is that we are powerful beyond measure...*
> *We ask ourselves: Who am I to be brilliant, gorgeous, talented, fabulous?*
> *Actually, who are you not to be?...*
> *As we let our light shine, we unconsciously give other people permission to do the same.*
> *As we are liberated from our own fear, our presence automatically liberates others.*

How relevant this wonderful quotation is to the singer and singing! The last two lines particularly relate to the power we wield as we perform.

It is often the case that singers are tremendously fearful of the power of singing, either its power to change the world and others or the power it may have to change *them*. It may lead a singer to places inside she would rather not go, where she may discover pains or wounds that she would rather not face. This is the aspect of singing's power I am particularly concerned with in this book. When I ask you to allow yourself to find your authentic voice, I realize that it can be a fearful prospect when we understand the visceral connection singing has to our own power and emotions.

Perhaps we are afraid of our power and our possibilities because by using them we commit ourselves to an unfamiliar path that may prove very demanding; we are uncertain where it will lead us. But seizing power means we must take responsibility for our action and accept the consequences. Singing may change your life or someone else's; it may even change the world and that takes courage! *But to be fully ourselves, we must follow this path.* It is my belief that our unhappiness stems from *not* fully realizing our potential and not following our world-changing path. I also believe that deep down, beyond the ego, in our authentic core, we *know* that.

WHAT IT TAKES TO SING

It is essential, then, to acknowledge every aspect of the power of singing, so that we don't underestimate the power *we need to draw on* to sing. If we see singing as relevant, important, healing, potentially life changing, or providing an empathic voice for our listeners, we will be willing to commit our energy to it. How could we not? If we dismiss it as a pastime or an insignificant, inessential part of our lives *or others' lives*, we will be unwilling to tap into the strength we need to be the best singer we can be. Why should we squander our energy if we don't see our singing as powerful and transformative? Also remember: if we, as singers, underestimate singing's power, how can we expect our listeners to take us seriously? And if they don't take us seriously, why should they listen or go even further and make themselves vulnerable by opening themselves up to receiving our gift?

Imagine if, when we are performing, the voices in our heads were constantly saying, "I know this isn't important and has no significance for you at all, but I want to sing it anyway because I like it. It's sort of pretty, and I want affirmation of my worth." Our performance would be halfhearted at best. As listeners, we have probably all experienced such a performance and wondered why we came away feeling so empty.

As we have already acknowledged, the power of the singing voice is no less profound for the listener: he will experience memory stimulation and emotional recall, sympathetic vibration in his own body, and feel the connection to his own breath, his life energy. *But this can only happen if we take him there through our own belief in that power.*

In regularly reminding ourselves of the power of singing, we program into our psyches and our bodies the idea that singing has value. We assure ourselves of singing's worth in order *not to deny our voices the power they intrinsically hold.* At the same time we show our audience respect by presenting them with our best because when we know the power we hold, we can do nothing less.

Softly, in the dusk, a woman is singing to me;
Taking me back down the vista of years, till I see
A child sitting under the piano, in the boom of the tingling strings
And pressing the small, poised feet of a mother who smiles as she sings.

In spite of myself, the insidious mastery of song
Betrays me back, till the heart of me weeps to belong
To the old Sunday evenings at home, with the winter outside
And hymns in the cosy parlour, the tinkling piano our guide.

So now it is vain for the singer to burst into clamour
With the great black piano appassionato. The glamour
Of childish days is upon me, my manhood is cast
Down in the flood of remembrance,

I weep like a child for the past. – D.H. Lawrence, *"Piano"*

Ways to Acknowledge Your Power:

- *First, it is vitally important that you yourself recognize the impor-tance and power of singing.* If you are still in doubt, you must say to yourself every time you sing "This is a power-ful means of expression of myself, my experience, and my emotions. Singing this song has the possibility to change me, others, and even the world. I will not squander its gift." If you are singing simply for your own pleasure, take time to focus on the pleasure it is giving you at that moment. Whether you're singing in the shower, as you do housework, or while on a walk, become aware of the power of singing. Do not allow yourself to take singing for granted or subordinate its possibilities.

- *Remember the empathic nature of singing.* As you are performing a song, be aware of the bond of empathy you are creating and allow your energy to flow toward your audience as if they are friends in need of support or patients in need of healing.

- *Become an advocate and an ambassador of singing and its power.* Talk to people about how singing can change our percep-tion of life or our experience of emotions or even transform the world. Initiate discussions with other people about their favorite songs, their memories of songs, and the emotions songs have inspired, and share with them the importance of singing in your life. Introduce other people to different styles of music and ask them to share favorite songs with you. Broaden your own and other people's perception of singing and turn their attention back to listening rather than simply letting songs "wash over" them.

- *Notice singing in every aspect of your life.* Make a mental note of every context in which singing appears, for example, on TV, at work, in church, in restaurants, on the radio, in the concert hall, walking in the mall, or in ceremonies. Pay attention to singing in the world.

- *Be aware of how singing draws people together.* Notice how it creates a sense of community for both performers and listeners and the profound effect that cooperation can have on your relationships with others. Begin to see singing as a vital social tool.

- *Acknowledge the magic.* Choose to take on the role of magician and use your powers to transform your listeners' lives. Whenever you perform, remind yourself of the spell you must cast as soon as you walk on stage. Feel the magic reach into the audience as you sing and keep its power energized even as you receive applause.

- *Put singing to the test.* When you feel low or sad or lack energy, try singing an upbeat song as loudly as possible or try soothing yourself with a beautiful lullaby. See how you change the mood of a group of people by playing a recording of, for instance, *Carmina Burana* by Carl Orff or the last movement of Beethoven's Ninth Symphony. There are hundreds of different ways to test the power of singing, and I encourage you to test a few on yourself or friends and observe the results!

The nineteenth-century German writer Goethe said "Whatever you can do or dream you can, begin it. Boldness has genius, power, and magic in it." The boldness to lead you to the "genius, power, and magic" in singing begins with belief in yourself and the knowledge that singing has the power to positively influence the lives of others and even transform the world. Our authentic voice expresses our humanity and our experience of the world. On hearing that voice, people will recognize themselves in it and understand our commonality. The power of singing is great indeed.

Realize the power of singing in your life.

CHAPTER 2

THE INSIGHT STORY

EMBARKING ON THE PATH TO SELF-DISCOVERY

When we get out of the glass bottle of our ego,
and when we escape like squirrels turning in the
cages of our personality
and get into the forest again,
we shall shiver with cold and fright.
But things will happen to us
so that we don't know our selves.

Cool, unlying life will rush in,
and passion will make our bodies taut with power,
we shall stamp our feet with new power
and old things will fall down,
we shall laugh, and institutions will curl up like
burnt paper.

– D.H. Lawrence, *"Escape"*

I once had a student who seemed to have everything anyone could ever desire. She was young and beautiful and married to an extremely successful surgeon who earned more money than they could ever spend. They had a dream house in the best neighborhood of town, a top-of-the-line SUV and a Jaguar in the garage, two beautiful children (and a nanny to take care of them), and exotic vacations whenever they wanted them. She was on various boards, did charity work, and helped with fund-raising for various institutions.

But she came to me because she was unhappy. Something was missing in her life. She had tried taking up painting and been moderately successful, but she was still dissatisfied. So she had looked deep inside and concluded that what she *really* wanted to do was to be a singer. Yes, that would bring her the elusive contentment she sought. So she began voice lessons.

The voice she came to me with was an unexceptional soprano, but one that could certainly have been a usable instrument for certain types of music with some work. Attempting to pay her way to fast success, she began three hours of voice lessons a week. Her logic told her that if she took three times the normal number of lessons, she could be ready for stardom and success three times as fast. I tried to explain that usually one can't rush these things, but she disguised her impatience as dedication, and I was curious to try such intensive work with someone.

Her expectation was that I would transform her, but it wasn't entirely up to me. She hadn't bargained for the fact that she had to work not only on technique and control but on herself. To change the sound that was coming out of her mouth, *she* had to change. She had expected me to hand her singing success on a plate through a list of simple guidelines—do this or stop doing that. A voice lesson often sounds just like that, but the actions connected to "doing this" and "not doing that" are frequently linked to such ingrained parts of ourselves that we can't simply change what we're doing on command. We have to discover *why* we cling to our habits so doggedly in order to change the source of the problem rather than papering over the cracks. I led her very gently and reassured her that I would be there to lean on when she was confronted with truths inside herself.

But the risks were too great. As soon as my student realized she couldn't just be "made" into a good singer and that she would have to put some of herself into the process, be conscious, change some very ingrained habits, look into herself, and maybe even question her life's choices so far, she quit. She hadn't bargained for the work happiness might take. She had wanted to put on the mantle of a singer like she put on her mink coat.

The problem this particular student had, in common with many others, was a fear of the self-discovery to which authentic singing can so often lead. I had begun to show her the path, but she didn't dare go down it.

UNDERSTANDING OUR INHIBITIONS

Throughout our lives, behind our tethered, restricted voices we may be hiding who we truly are and what we truly feel. In the beginning, as uninhibited babies, we are unafraid to express anything and happy to demand everything, with gurgles and cries that parents learn to interpret. As we grow, our voices of need and emotion are gradually silenced, either by social demand or by a controlling other (parent, friend, or partner), and we begin to inhibit communication of ourselves through our voices. We stop saying much of what we think or feel for fear of retribution, criticism, or of appearing foolish. Our voices become full of apprehension, manifested as self-control, and take on a disguise, often expressing what we think people want to hear but not who we truly are.

I believe one of the reasons singing has such universal appeal is that it gives us back permission to express our true selves and our authentic emotions. Singing, we can become like a child again, sending out to the world on our breath all those emotions that have been locked inside for so long because sharing them in any other circumstance would make us totally vulnerable and expose our weaknesses.

This sounds like an ideal possibility: sing and be real, sing and allow yourself to feel what you haven't dared to feel, sing and share what you really believe, sing and discover your true self. Isn't that what we all want? What a gift singing is! So why don't we all sing freely? Because once we are committed so completely to hiding ourselves and have created a life in which we don't have to be real or face our fears or feel anything fully, we don't want to be reminded of our subterfuge or open the door to facing it. Singing freely, I can assure you, will open that door, and we will have to confront ourselves. It is part of the wonderful gift of singing. And in doing so there is the real possibility that in finding the joy and happiness we seek through singing, we have to be prepared to deal with the pain and sorrow that is the opposite side of that coin. Authentic singing is powerful enough to expose it all and does not discriminate between the emotions it uncovers. For many that is a very scary proposition.

My student couldn't risk looking at herself because she would have had to look at all the "stuff" in her life and evaluate it. Maybe she would have to admit that there were things in her life that had to be given up before she could find her happiness. But her view of herself was intricately tied to that "stuff" since she viewed herself through the eyes of her friends, her family, and society in general, and it was all those trappings that gave her self-worth. But they didn't give her happiness. She was destined to leap from one "hobby" to another trying to discover herself, but each time failing because she was looking outward not inward. She was not prepared to change. She was afraid to come face-to-face with her true self.

DIGGING DEEP

On my journey, I have realized that at the root of great singing are qualities and beliefs that must be manifest *before* we can apply even the most finely honed technical skills. Most singers go to a voice teacher thinking that learning *how* to sing, that is, learning how to extend the range, control tone color, articulate the words, negotiate the leaps and runs, and generally take full control of the voice, will make them into great singers. But the key is not *how* but *why*. Where our desire to sing comes from has a profound effect on the singer we project to the world, on the results we experience, on the singer we develop into, and, ultimately, on our success.

MEET YOUR AUTHENTIC SINGER

It is my belief that there are three types of singers in the world, all motivated to sing for different reasons. Let me introduce them:

- *The Diva* sings to be loved and adored, to attract attention, for approval, and/or for power. Fame and wealth may also be on the Diva's list of reasons for wanting to sing, though don't think that Divas are necessarily only found in the realm of stars or solo singers. There can be Divas tucked away in choirs or groups where they often dominate in rehearsal, singing one dynamic step louder than everyone else and creating blending problems for the director or holding final high notes just a little too long. In general, the Diva lacks humility and is afraid to admit her weaknesses for fear she would dent her highly developed ego.

- *The Introvert* sings as a means of escape from shyness and a way to share feelings and emotions with the world in a safe environment. Singing becomes a disguise that allows the Introvert to hide behind the veil of the song; he can always remind the world that singing is just acting, a pretense— or so he would have us believe. Singing gives the Introvert a safe outlet for the hidden emotion that otherwise would never see light of day and without having to take full ownership of it. Singing also offers the Introvert a safe place to create the connection with others that he craves but finds so difficult to achieve in everyday life. But don't be fooled by outward demeanor: while the Introvert's ego is somewhat fragile, it is still the driving force. His insecurities often manifest in false modesty that is only thinly disguised as humility.

- *The Authentic Singer* sings from a desire to share experiences with the world, give something meaningful to others, empathize, and/or simply to sing (for instance, when we sing in the shower, we all become Authentic Singers). Authentic Singers sing from the inside out; because the singing is reward enough, they give little thought to the possible return. They may enjoy feeling the vibrations in their bodies; they may sing particular songs because they move them to add their own creative voice or because they want others to experience what they have learned from life or felt through a song. They sing from their souls. They give generously of themselves to their listeners with no demand for return. They sing with humility and courage.

You may recognize each of these types in someone you know or someone you've seen or heard perform. No doubt you see one of them in yourself (be honest about it!).

My own belief is that *there are all three singers inside everyone.* Consider this:

- We all want to be loved and appreciated, and have power and control over things (*the Diva*).
- We can all feel very vulnerable and shy and "stuck" in our emotions at times, needing to find an outlet, or long for honest relationships with others (*the Introvert*).
- We all have experiences so moving that we would like to share them with others, or find ourselves singing just to feel good or *because* we feel good (*the Authentic Singer*).

There is nothing inherently wrong with the first two types, and I will talk in chapter 9 about their usefulness. But although we may feel we get something out of each one of these singers, the Authentic Singer is the only one *anyone else* wants to hear and the only one that will lead us down the path to great singing and the greatest satisfaction and fulfillment. Only when we sing authentically, giving from our hearts and our souls, are we able to share ourselves and our experiences with our audience, moving and even changing them. Only as the Authentic Singer do we get our egos out of the way of the song in order to give it its full power. It is the Authentic Singer who *confronts us with ourselves.* My student in the above story was terrified to uncover what her Authentic Singer would reveal. She wanted to stay the Diva or the Introvert because she wanted singing to feed her and fix her but was not prepared to offer either herself or her listeners honesty and trust.

The Diva and the Introvert are simply two sides of our ego. For those who have been so dominated by these ego-driven characters, it may seem an impossible task to ignore their demands and allow the Authentic Singer to take center stage. The Diva and the Introvert are voracious in their needs. But when we look carefully, the Authentic Voice is the only one to which we can effectively attend. After all, giving and sharing are completely under our control, whereas what we are given back is up to others, out of our control and unpredictable. When the Diva and the

Introvert demand a return from their listeners, they *relinquish* control. The important thing to realize here is that by singing from our true selves, by making our purpose giving and sharing not needing and taking, we open the door to receiving exactly what our Diva and our Introvert want—love, adoration, appreciation, and power for the one, and freedom to speak out and connect for the other.

If we want to improve our singing experience, our aim should be to push the Diva and the Introvert into the background and focus on developing our Authentic Singer. If we ignore it and let the ego voices dominate, then we run the risk of handing over control of our singing life to other people, and why would we want to do that?

WHERE DID OUR FREE VOICE GO?

Many factors along our path serve to stifle our true, free voice. We all begin on our journey with the same possibilities, but because of physical makeup, we have different (and unique) qualities inherent in our voices. One voice may be richer, bigger, deeper, higher, or brighter than another. But we all have the possibility to express ourselves very successfully through our singing voices.

In Zimbabwe they have a saying "If you can walk you can dance; if you can talk you can sing." I truly believe that. However, often, very early on our singing journey, we come to crossroads where we are required to make decisions about our voices; a misguided choice at that point then sends us along the wrong path without us even realizing it. A few more wrong choices at the next few crossroads will set us off on a mazelike path from which it becomes more and more complicated to extricate ourselves. Sound familiar?

The choices I'm talking about may be physical ("I feel like I might run out of breath so I'll help out by holding my jaw and tightening my throat...") or emotional ("I'm afraid to sound bad, so I'll sing as softly as I can and not attempt the high notes") or pragmatic ("My friend is singing alto in choir, so I think I will too"). The decisions may be consciously or unconsciously made when we are such inexperienced travelers, but nevertheless we are tying the knots that make up our singing future.

Sometimes our choices are influenced far too much by outside opinion. A young student may feel great when her peers cheer her on in her imitation of a favorite rock singer, but by continuing without guidance, she could create bad habits that lead her to suffer vocal nodules and a life of vocal problems. Several of my older students have stories of being forbidden from singing in class at a young age because the choir teacher said that they had no voice or couldn't keep the tune. They have told me of their embarrassment and horror at that moment and that they haven't dared open their mouths to sing since. With a little instruction, however, they have learned to control their voices, carry the melody, and find immense enjoyment from singing. Now they express their regret at not having dared to do this earlier. How often I have heard "If only I'd done this when I was twenty!" Their choice then was to relinquish power to a less-than-enlightened teacher—something that is so easy to do when you are young and inexperienced.

Wrong choices on our singing path are not only for the inexperienced. I had a very good friend who was a successful opera singer with a lucrative, full-time contract singing in an opera house in Germany. He sang leading roles for fifteen years before he woke up one day to find his voice range reduced to five notes. It turned out that although he had taken years of voice lessons, he had not been applying the principles of healthy vocal technique, and the demands of his taxing schedule caught up with him. Using the "wrong" muscles constantly and ignoring any warning signs eventually meant his voice one day said simply "enough is enough" and gave up on him. As a result he had to go back to train with a new teacher and spent the next two years recreating his voice. He never sang on an opera stage again.

It is so easy to create these knots, but it can be extremely painful to unravel them. But we need to do so if we are to come face to face once more with our free voices.

The Natural Singer

We have all heard about singers who sing naturally; these are people who have never had a voice lesson in their lives and yet sing like angels. "She was born singing like that," I've heard people say. I used to believe that these "natural" singers were just incredible listeners and imitators, who felt in their bodies what other great singers did (singers who *had* done the work and taken the lessons!) and copied it. I gave them full marks for imitating and zero for effort or understanding. Perhaps that is to some extent true, but I think I was selling them short. I now believe most of these people are singers who have made the right choices at their crossroads (consciously or unconsciously), and for whatever reasons have always sung freely and authentically. They are probably extremely instinctive and *feel* what is right for them; they are more likely to be listening to their own inner voice than to someone else's external instrument or following others' bad advice. They are led by the Authentic Singer.

Of course, not all natural singers push themselves to the extremes that some of us might challenge ourselves to go or use their instruments to the full. Some may choose to stay within a very safe range vocally and emotionally. But what they do is real, free, and true to themselves.

Many ethnic/folk singers all over the world may fit this definition. Think of singers of African, Celtic, bluegrass, Spanish flamenco, Portuguese fado or any native folk vocal traditions. These are people expressing to the world their experience of it: they sing about the Appalachian Mountains or the life of a child in Botswana or the way love manifests itself in Spain. Or they just tell a story. They sing because they want everyone to know, understand, and in some small way share their experience of their world. This particular sort of natural, mostly untrained singing is not unique to the folk world, and such singers are not necessarily "more authentic" than those from other genres or those who are highly trained in their art. But what we see here is authenticity laid bare, the true self unselfconsciously paraded. *That* part of the "natural" or "folk" singer's art is the part we should all be looking to emulate; we should not allow it to be overshadowed by overemphasis on technique and show.

FINDING YOUR AUTHENTIC CORE

Finding the Authentic Singer means chipping away at everything that is inhibiting its emergence, as Michelangelo talked of chipping away at a piece of marble to find the beautiful statue within. This involves digging through psychological, as well as physical baggage. You must be prepared to change physical habits. You must also be prepared to look closely at what you think, believe, and feel, and then change some mental habits. You must become flexible in your approach, looking at things from the inside and the outside, and perhaps even be prepared to forget what you have imagined singing to be like up until now. Let go of your expectations and give yourself permission to make all sorts of sounds you never imagined yourself making. Stop judging and start experiencing.

I will go into all these aspects of getting to the heart of singing in the chapters that follow, but for now, here are a few suggestions to get you started on your path.

LAUNCHING YOURSELF ON THE PATH TO SELF-DISCOVERY:

- *First of all, just SING!* Find songs you love and that you connect with emotionally. If they make you cry, all the better; if they make you joyful, great. Make a list of all the songs you love and that have an effect on you in one way or other. Keep adding to it as you hear new songs or remember old ones. Discover what it is about a song that really makes you *feel* something. Don't sing songs to dance to unless they make you so brimful of joy that you can't help but dance. If you hear a choir singing a song that moves you, get a recording and sing along. Above all, avoid staying safe. By focusing on what a song is all about and why you love it so much, your singing can take you to emotional places you weren't even aware it could take you. *Allow* yourself to feel - as deeply as possible. Begin to experience your own emotions right there in the open and let the vibrations you create in your own body when you sing enhance the sensations. Make singing any song *a conscious process*, physically and mentally.

- *Read texts of songs as if reading a poem or story.* Say them out loud. Think about what it means and how you feel about what the song expresses through the words. Make a decision only to sing songs that have words you feel connected to. Don't allow the words of a song simply to wash over you without considering their meaning. If you sing songs in foreign languages, make sure you know exactly what you are singing about, and open yourself up to the emotional world of a different culture. When I talk about emotions, I don't just mean highly charged or sad or sentimental; songs might make you laugh out loud or just smile or sigh when you first read through them. That's wonderful! In fact, start a collection of songs that cover the broadest emotional range and sing them often. Keep adding to your repertoire and digging into different parts of yourself.

- *Listen to styles of singing that are unfamiliar to you.* Be as broad as possible: classical, jazz, musicals, opera, rock, pop, bluegrass, gospel, folk, Celtic, chants, and choral. Immerse yourself in song and stay open to its effect on you. Ask yourself why you like one style over another. Discover the shared elements of songs from different genres that you like. Can you name what it is that moves you? Analyze songs intellectually but then be prepared to fully connect to them emotionally. Ask yourself these questions: What memories does this revive? What different feelings am I experiencing? Why would I want other people to share this? What insight can I bring to them? Write things down if necessary. When you discover the truth behind your emotional response to the songs, you begin to find the path to your true self. You begin to be able to truly express your *self* in song.

- *Join a choir.* Determine to suppress your Diva by fully committing to sharing your talent in a group situation, paying attention to becoming part of the group, not standing outside of it, and not pushing to be a star. Hand over control and learn to fit in. Allow your Introvert to find support by singing with others where your vulnerability is minimized, and you can safely try out new things without being too exposed. Learn the joy of singing when you take all pressure off yourself to be "perfect" and focus on the music itself. Discover the sense of fulfillment you can get from teamwork and being a supportive member of a group.

- *Recognize and encourage the motivations of your Authentic Singer.* Look to why you want to sing, why you sing what you sing, and why you want to share what you sing. Stay honest with yourself but be aware that the intent of your three singers may be battling for priority. It is up to you to deny the Diva and the Introvert the power to lead your actions. Ask yourself:

  What motivates me to sing?
  Who am I singing for?
  What will my audience get out my performance?
  What am I giving my listener?
  What do I hope for or expect in return?
  Determine to nurture generosity and giving as the motivator of your intent.

- *Notice the Diva or Introvert moments.* Acknowledge, without judgment, moments when your overriding need is to feed or satisfy or protect your ego. For instance, you may notice yourself wondering if a family member is listening to you practice and whether they will think you sound good or not. You may adjust what you are practicing to show yourself in the best light. Or you may notice yourself singing one dynamic step softer than everyone else in the choir in case you make a mistake, or you may sing a step louder to be noticed. Or you may feel yourself withholding your emotional commitment to a song for fear of looking foolish. Become aware of these moments. Then begin to identify underlying *authentic* reasons for singing and try to make these your motivation. Say to yourself "My aim is to do justice to this song, enjoy the experience of it, and be fully involved in it" or "I want my listeners to understand how beautiful/powerful this song is." Once you start to do this regularly, you'll begin to understand who this Authentic Singer is, help him grow, and diminish the power of those other ego-centered characters in your singing life who only block your path and inhibit discovery of your full potential as a singer.

Become aware of the Authentic Singer within.

CHAPTER 3

TAKING THE PLUNGE

UNDERSTANDING COMMITMENT

"Great art plays for mortal stakes" – Robert Frost

To be the singer we want to be, we must learn how to commit ourselves fully to our art and not be afraid of the risks that involves. Underneath it all, that is what we expect of ourselves, and we will not be fully satisfied with anything less. When we are not committed, we provide ourselves with the weakest excuse for failure—that we haven't done everything we are capable of to be a success. By not being fully committed, we create dissatisfaction for our listeners and ourselves. But understanding what commitment feels like is elusive for many singers.

Maybe we should begin by asking what does commitment *sound* like?

Beauty is in the eye of the beholder, the saying goes, and it is certainly true of singing that beauty is in the ear of the listener. In fact it is remarkable how singers of widely diverse qualities appeal to different people. We can all think of favorite singers who have inspired us in our own singing life. Maybe if you sing classical music your list includes Joan Sutherland, Luciano Pavarotti, Renée Fleming, Anne-Sophie von Otter, or Bryn Terfel. Perhaps jazz/blues lovers would include Ella Fitzgerald, Joe Williams, Koko Taylor, or Billie Holliday. Your personal favorites might be Frank Sinatra, Stevie Wonder, Joni Mitchell, Barbra Streisand, Al Green, James Taylor, Eva Cassidy, or David Gray; if you delve into more eclectic spheres of music you may think of Loreena McKennit, Ute Lempe, Natalie Merchant, or Joao Gilberto. Your list could include Janis Joplin, Mick Jagger, Bob Dylan, Louis Armstrong, or many more whose voices we don't necessarily associate with the adjective *beautiful.* Yet think what an enormous hit

Armstrong had with his truly beautiful and moving rendition of "What a Wonderful World." Who doesn't smile and feel good when they hear it?

When I consider the wide array of successful singers, I am struck by the vast differences in *technical* mastery from one singer to another. By technical mastery I mean the control of breath, use of range and color, flexibility, agility, and beauty of tone. Some use their voices to the full extent of their range and power, pushing themselves to the edge of physical and vocal possibilities. Like a great violinist, they have studied and honed their craft to a phenomenal degree of control, beauty, and expression. But not all great singers have, or at least utilize, such technical skill. I would even venture to suggest that quite a number of highly successful singing stars know little or nothing about vocal technique or healthy use of their instruments[4]. Some may sing within an octave range (or less), off pitch, with a rough sound and barely any breath control. Certain styles make different requirements of the artist and even *demand* a different technical approach, but the gap in skill levels is remarkable.

Singers, as far as I can see, are unique in this. There's not a fiddler in the world that would get much further than the street corner playing out of tune on only one string! I am not seeking to imply that any of these singers aren't great musicians or accomplished performers. Nor am I suggesting the superiority of one singer or genre over another. I am simply pointing out the anomaly that when it comes to singing and singers, what the average listener responds to has nothing necessarily to do with *technical* skill.

So what *is* the secret of the singer's success? How do we reconcile some singers' vocal limitations with their success? The key is *commitment*. In the greatest singers, the audience senses the singers' complete immersion in the performance—the total commitment of energy, emotion, and thought to the act of singing and communicating the song. It involves giving not taking. That is as true for the great pop star as it is for the great opera singer. Commitment is, in fact, *the essence* of singing success; it's the one *essential* ingredient we cannot do without, and the one

---

4   The large number of pop/rock artists seeking help and remedy for nodules and vocal stress problems bears this out.

thing any audience craves. Janis Joplin once said, "If I hold back, I'm no good. I'd rather be good sometimes than holding back all the time." Whether or not you love her, when you listen to Joplin sing, you certainly can't deny her commitment. No matter what the consequences might be, she didn't "hold back"; that was the root of her success, and she knew it. Perhaps she was less aware that in committing so fully, she became good all the time. Commitment, pure and simple, was what her audience was there to feel.

Successful singers have recognized that there is an audience out there who will find *their commitment* relevant, whether it comes with highly skilled technique or not. Listeners respond differently to different voices; some like a voice that is beautiful, but others want to hear a voice that sounds more like their own or one that has a "pure," untrained sound. Some enjoy a voice that embodies passion; some want to hear a sound that conveys the struggles of their own lives. Here is another example of the empathy of singing: the reflection back to the listener of something he recognizes and understands. The successful singer, then, is the one willing to commit himself to communicating in whatever way necessary to have his voice heard. In other words, he is prepared to risk freeing his Authentic Singer.

Why Do We Resist?

The heroism we recite
Would be a daily thing,
Did not ourselves the cubits warp
For fear to be a king.
— Emily Dickinson

The question is why do we resist committing ourselves fully to any of the aspects necessary to becoming the best singer we can be? Why do we not just get on with it? The first and probably most powerful reason is fear. But there are other factors that may come into play, so let's take a look at all the issues that may lead us to compromise our commitment.

- **Fear of Failure**

  As I have already mentioned, singing is a very personal expression of our deepest self and exposing that to others or ourselves is never going to be easy or risk free. There are also a million and one technical things that we know could go wrong and cause us to appear foolish or imperfect. *What if I run out of air? What if that high note cracks? What if no sound comes out? What if I sing off pitch? What if I forget the words? What if my throat closes up, and I end up sounding like a strangled cat?* Yes, we know that anything could happen, and our friendly little devil voice will remind us every time how ugly some of those possibilities could be. This is the Fear of Failure that haunts almost every singer I know.

  You may have several less-than-helpful responses to this hovering specter:

  - You may anticipate your own failure and deliberately deny yourself the possibility of success by not fully committing yourself to the task.
  - You may stick rigidly to a very narrow range of possibility where you know you are safe.
  - You may deny your weaknesses and not even explore new possibilities in your practice because change itself is too much of a risk.

- **Fear of Success**

  Failure may not be our only fear. We must also recognize that the fear of *success* may be a factor in our lack of commitment. Along with success in singing comes a huge responsibility. We "fear to be a king," as Emily Dickinson said.

  I have already talked about the power of singing, and if we take that seriously, then our burden as singers is great. We cannot dismiss singing as irrelevant if we believe in the power it wields. Its importance weighs on us whether because we care so much about what we are saying and giving (our Authentic Singer) or because our self-worth rests upon it (the Diva emerging). And the more successful we are, the more weight we carry to the next performance. Our fears are constantly compounded. (Could this sort of burden be partly responsible for the meltdown of certain famous performers we see so publicly displayed in the tabloids?) If we fear what will happen, the work we have to do, or the power we may unleash, of course our commitment will be compromised. We hold back because we are afraid of what changes and demands success may bring. We are afraid of the responsibility.

- **Laziness**
  We could simply be lazy when it comes to our singing. We don't want to put in the work, either physical or mental, to make our voices the best they can be. Many singers who are lazy charge their lack of success to anything else, simply because they don't want to face the fact that perhaps working harder will get them where they want to be. Only you can know if this is the case for you.

- **Ambivalence**
  We may be ambivalent toward our singing. Could we cope with success? Do we care enough? Is it really what we want right now? Sometimes we have not thought enough about singing to even know what we want. We may need to focus on exactly what we are asking of ourselves and ask more questions about our ambitions before we can fully commit to doing whatever it takes to improve.

- **Overconfidence**
  Occasionally overconfidence can be a barrier to full commitment. There may be some readers who say "I've never had a problem with fear in my singing. I've always just loved showing off my talent!" There are such singers around, and I have come across a few. So you would think that without fear they would be able to tread the path to very rapid success, fully able to allow the Authentic Singer to sing, uninhibited by doubt. Some do—if they are Authentic Singers already. However, the problem for such a singer is that often the Diva is in fact hiding his fears under an *illusion* of confidence. Safety is created

by a *pretense* of fearlessness and lack of self-analysis. His self-confident bluster then masks flaws of which the singer remains blissfully ignorant but which nevertheless prove to be obstacles in his path to singing success. Most of these singers are closed to suggestions for improvement from anyone, even their voice teachers. (Yes, I've had one or two students like this who have come to me thinking they already know everything.) For singers in this category, the key is to acknowledge their problem, learn to balance confidence with humility, admit to the need for growth and change, and in so doing, take a long hard look at where their fears may be hiding and draw them out. Fear needs confronting in order to clear the path forward.

Ironically, for the most part, the solution to all the above obstacles is *full commitment* to our singing path. What we are unaware of is that by not applying ourselves 100 percent to the task at hand, we *create* the fears that prevent us from making a commitment! So commitment itself needs our full attention and our understanding of what it involves if we are to achieve success.

WHAT DO WE HAVE TO COMMIT TO?

When I talk about commitment I am not talking only about your commitment simply to being a singer, not just the "big picture." I'm talking about commitment right down to the smallest detail. It is not enough to simply learn the notes and words in time for the concert. That is only part of what you have to do. Commitment shows up in the learning, the technique, the approach to the words and the music, the emotional involvement, the attitude to the listener, the dedication to communication, and all the other details that contribute to the outcome.

From a broad perspective, the manifestations of commitment in singing can be grouped into two areas—the emotional aspect, governed by right-brain function, and the technical aspect, governed for the most part by left-brain function. Both areas need to be attended to and balanced. Let us look at what commitment means from the standpoint of these two factors.

Emotional Commitment

This might be said to be the baring of one's soul through the singing of the song. Singing is our opportunity to connect to emotions we normally may not dare to confront, and this may be one of the reasons that so many people want to sing. Yet fear of that confrontation makes such commitment is extremely difficult.

In the rock world this sort of commitment counts for everything; for a rock singer, technical considerations are minor if he is prepared to throw caution to the wind and allow his authentic voice to be heard. For the listener, this singing, aided by the persistent drumbeat and frenzied body movements that may accompany it, harkens back to the very core of our selves. It returns us to our raw emotions, away from our intellect, back to our passions. It connects us to the emotional power within every one of us while relaxing our need to control or inhibit ourselves. Think of the audience at a rock concert. What hooks them? Partly it must be the excitement of watching and hearing performers take all the risks they themselves dare not take. At a certain moment, the audience itself begins letting go and experiencing the freedom of expression that reverberates through the music, and, in the safety of a crowd of strangers, powerful emotions can be released. Many people will come away from a rock concert with a feeling of exhilaration, excitement, and even extreme joy.

It was watching the PBS TV series "Ken Burn's Jazz" that made me think that the addiction in popular Western culture to this raw emotional commitment began with the emergence of the swing bands of the fifties. Of course, emotional commitment had been there in some form in every other style of music: in opera since its inception in the seventeenth century, in folk music from every land, and of course in the blues and jazz of the early twentieth century. But it was when jazz was really out in the open and people started dancing to it and participating in it themselves that the man in the street began to feel the true emotional connection he could find through music, particularly songs. People began to clamor for songs that made them *feel* not *think*. Later, rock and heavy metal bands were to tap into this visceral quality to the extreme, using pounding beats and turning up the volume to such a degree that their listeners were forced to literally *feel* the music. Singers now had to turn up the volume of their singing too, pouring out raw emotions through their voices.

For an untrained or undisciplined singer, this type of commitment brings with it the possibility of damage to the voice. Powerful, authentic feelings that begin benignly enough deep in the belly may transform into throat-locking, breath-denying energy as they try to emerge through the voice. Think of the lump in the throat we experience as we're about to cry, or the way our voices may tighten or even disappear in moments of anger or frustration. Our emotions are directly connected to our expression of them through the voice. If we have any fear or doubt or restriction attached to those feelings, which we almost always do since they are well programmed by the society we live in, it will be reflected in our voices; they will be inhibited, strangled, or weakened. To compensate, we may force the voice, pushing from the throat, tightening the shoulders, tensing the tongue, holding the jaw, and upsetting the delicate vocal balance. Our emotions, if we are not careful, sabotage our efforts to express them by closing down, rather than opening up, vocal possibilities. Without technical understanding or attention to the delicacy of the muscles involved, vocal burnout and tremendous strain results.

Although as far as many people in an audience are concerned, this sort of emotional commitment is enough to hook them, it can turn out to be very unhealthy for the singer and lead to a short-lived career. If we are to express ourselves fully and freely through our voices, and extend our singing life and possibilities, we must combine emotional commitment with technical understanding.

COMMITMENT TO TECHNIQUE

Vocal technique is what should result from understanding the vocal mechanism, regular practice, and familiarity with one's own vocal possibilities. But it is no good *knowing* that lifting your soft palate will create the sound you want for a particular phrase if you don't *commit* yourself to doing it every time.

I had a student who was an excellent singer when performing classical songs. Her phrasing, breath control, and beauty of tone in songs by Brahms or Fauré or Vaughn Williams were the envy of many other accomplished singers. One day she had the opportunity to sing with a jazz band and decided to venture into the realm of Gershwin, Cole Porter, and Jerome Kern. I was taken aback when she presented the first number, "So in Love." Her technique fell apart, and she seemed to have no support for shaping phrases or coloring tone. Her performance was dull, and she was constantly under pitch and regularly running out of air. I asked her what she thought of her own performance. "I don't seem to have control of the song at all," she said. "And I thought this would be so much easier than Brahms!"

What she had done was not so much underestimate the difficulty of the pieces, but rather she had not realized that *all* songs, whatever their seeming level of difficulty, will fall apart without commitment to technique, especially commitment to *using the breath.* She told me she thought that songs like this should sound relaxed and easy, so in her mind she had translated that to don't work so hard. That thought had then resulted in sloppy technique and collapse of vital vocal support, which caused every problem in the book!

Happily my student's problems solved themselves when she understood their root. Through her understanding of the vocal mechanism, breath management, and resonance, she was able to discover how to fully commit herself to her technique while still staying true to the style of the song. Adjusting what she was doing technically (changing the vowels shapes, using alternate vocal colors, etc) didn't mean relinquishing her commitment to singing well.

For some singers a complete change of style (e.g. classical to pop) must be approached with a change of technique because what works technically for one style may not for another. To successfully negotiate such a transition, a singer may have to learn several different techniques for particular parts of her voice. For instance, a soprano may learn to use her chest voice somewhat higher in pop music than she would in opera; she may need to use "belt" technique as opposed to bel canto. A baritone may want to create a more conversational style and brighter tone in his musical theater role than in German Lieder, and he must learn how to achieve this by altering his technical approach. However, *all these techniques should be based on the same healthy roots.*

Some singers trying to make the transition between styles fail to understand this. Often they either know only one set of vocal habits, one way to sing any particular note or vowel, so everything sounds alike. Alternatively, they may overdo aspects of the style they are attempting. In the case of a pop singer trying to sing opera, he may exaggerate vowel shapes or tuck the chin way down to attempt a darker sound; a classical singer trying jazz, like my student in the story above, may drop her commitment to any technique to attempt to sound relaxed, so what is left is insipid and disconnected. Just as we can change tone color depending on emotional content, so it is also possible to mentally control technique depending on context. But what the singer must understand is that though technique may vary slightly from one style to another, *one's commitment to that technique does not.*

Hiding Behind Technique

There is a danger that may accompany the total commitment to technique that I've been discussing—focus on technique may distract us from or become a *substitute* for our emotional commitment. Don't forget that our fears are always looking for a good excuse for less than optimum commitment, and if we have an opportunity to shirk in the emotion department by dazzling our listeners with technique, why not take it? This problem is particularly evident among classical singers.

I remember vividly conversations among singers in the recreation room at my college; they were constantly comparing one singer's *mezza voce* against another's, talking of which famous tenor best negotiated the *passaggio,* and whether one singer's *coloratura* was clearer and faster than another's. Technical achievement was what it was all about. Even the technical words, the "singer speak" that sounded so erudite in its foreignness, seemed to be a way to avoid emotional connection to the performances discussed.

It is very easy to get distracted by technical prowess when what one is singing is technically extremely difficult. But we must not lose sight of the fact that technique is only a means to an end, with the end being the communication of the song by our Authentic Singer to stimulate an emotional response in our listeners.

I must add here that there is an audience that will go along with, appreciate, thoroughly enjoy, and even be transported by a purely technical performance. I am not trying to take anything away from fabulous technicians or their admirers. Such singing represents complete commitment of one sort and, as such, is to be applauded. As the rock singer commits emotionally and is successful, so a classical singer can do the same with technique, like a virtuoso violinist playing Paganini or a pianist playing Liszt. The technical commitment is total and so produces a very viable result.

But there is certainly plenty of evidence to show that technical skill partnered with emotional commitment produces a far more satisfying experience. Listen to opera singer Cecilia Bartoli singing Vivaldi's florid arias on her recording *The Vivaldi Album*, and you may be dazzled by her technical prowess, but it would be a far less exciting experience if it weren't for her equally committed emotional drive. We suddenly become aware what all those vocal acrobatics are expressing. How much more satisfying that is!

HIDING BEHIND THE VEIL OF IMAGE

Finding a way to avoid full commitment to the Authentic Singer by finding an alternative strategy of distraction is not only a trick of the technically minded classical singer. The equivalent for the pop/rock singer could be said to be her commitment to image. In these days of hastily made careers through shows like *American Idol*, the singer may be driven not by her Authentic Singer (though that may well be where she began) but by an outside team who create her image and a persona, which must be carefully and dedicatedly adhered to in order to sell the product that has been so quickly manufactured. Because there is an audience out there to appreciate this "product," the singer may be tempted to think it is enough just to live out this image—committed at least to that, but without the pain and fear of full emotional and technical commitment to her art. Creating such a false persona does not, however, lead the singer to satisfaction or happiness, nor does it lead to an authentic experience for most listeners. The careers of such singers are usually very short-lived.

I believe that to become the singer you really want to be, you cannot avoid total commitment to all aspects of singing. You must seek both emotional *and* technical commitment. That is the path to your greatest singing, whatever style you choose.

BREATH

In chapter 6, I will explain the vital importance of commitment to the breath. But for now I just want to remind you that it is through not trusting and so not fully committing our energies to our breath that we cause the problems that make our singing uncomfortable and restricted. As soon as the breath is not working 100 percent, *something else will take over* to make up for the missing essential energy. Stay conscious of full commitment to trusting your breath, as well as commitment to developing your breath capacity and control, so that it can be used to its greatest effect and fullest possibility.

ARTICULATION AND THE IMPORTANCE OF THE TEXT

Could mortal lip divine
The undeveloped freight
Of a delivered syllable,
'T would crumble with the weight.
                    – Emily Dickinson

As we have discussed, singing is a means of sharing ideas and experiences with others. What else are we as singers if we are not communicators? So we need to take a look at the main channel of communication in singing—the process of forming words. Our lack of commitment is often laid bare in this aspect of singing: if we do not make the words of our song clear, we cannot be committed to communicating all we need to through them.

In the world of music, singing is unique in its use of words. It is the words of a song that present a bridge to understanding of the music for the audience. Although abstract, instrumental music may well invoke powerful feelings, the familiarity of text is often a faster trigger of emotional response for many people because it relates directly to what they see as their real world.

For the singer-musician, words are an added dimension that, as well as being a huge aid to communication of ideas, feelings, and stories, can also present a minefield of potential problems. *Articulation* is the word we use to describe the mechanics of forming the words. If we don't articulate well enough for people to understand, communication is impeded and our full storytelling potential lost[5]. So, clear articulation must be part of our commitment when we sing. But because we use the same articulators[6] in speech, when it comes to singing those familiar muscles are often lethargic and unwilling to work as hard as they need to, since their job is now many times more demanding.

When we speak, we use a limited range of pitches and usually utilize a low to medium-low placement of our voices; articulation in speech generally entails moving very quickly from a consonant through the vowel and back to a consonant. Consonants become the primary distinguishing feature of words and the listener's key to meaning. In singing, however, the vowels take on new importance since they are the vehicles for the voice, the shapes through which the vibrating breath (now manifested as sound waves) passes to be transformed into musical sound, lingering for a determined length of time on a particular pitch. These shapes have an extremely important effect also on the quality of the sound: they determine whether the voice is beautiful, warm, shrill, edgy, rich, or thin. Since for most of us the sound of the voice is vitally important, careful attention must be paid to how we shape each vowel if we are to achieve our goal of communicating the meaning of the words through the sound we want.

---

5   I am not going to deal here with those singers who deliberately distort or obfuscate words for effect; that in the end is a matter of style choice that must be made with the awareness that the end product will then have to stand on its own as an abstract entity like instrumental music.

6   Simply put, the articulators in singing are the lips, tongue, jaw, soft palate, and cheek muscles.

I might add here that there are also differences between styles; the same word may be formed differently if we sing it in a pop song or an operatic aria. But, whatever the style, we must still fully commit ourselves to communication. So the singer must understand that the words with which he is so familiar in speech may "feel" quite different in his mouth and body when he begins to sing them. Commitment to this feeling of the words, as opposed to the one with which he is so familiar in speech, takes awareness and practice.

Ideally when we sing, the listener should *perceive* that the words we express are just like spoken words, even though the formation of them in the mouth may be altered from speech to accommodate pitch, tone, or resonance. However, your approach to those words may differ according to circumstances. Here are a few things to bear in mind when approaching articulation:

- *Remember the style.* The somewhat exaggerated, "received" pronunciation appropriate for the words in an English art song, for example, would be quite inappropriate for a jazz ballad. The exaggerated clarity of consonants necessary to cross the footlights for a song in musical theater would be out of place in a pop setting or intimate cabaret. Remind yourself that how the words are formed, particularly the shape of the vowels, has a profound effect on the tone produced, and a slightly inappropriately formed vowel can actually change the listener's sense of the style. Rich, round vowels may work perfectly well for classical arias but may be out of place in a brash, belted musical theater song. The subtle difference in formation is a lesson well learned, in whatever style you wish to sing.

- *A different level of energy is needed for consonants in a recording studio than in a concert hall.* Likewise if you are using a microphone, your attack will be gentler than if you are singing using only the natural acoustics of a hall. Beware, however, of lowering your *commitment*, thinking the mike will do the work for you—it won't!

- *Keep in mind your audience and the space in which they are listening.* The intimacy of someone's living room or the vastness of an opera house calls for a different level of energy to enable clear communication of the text.

- *Pay attention to the origin of the text.* A setting of words by Shakespeare such as "Sigh no more, Ladies" would demand different vowel formation than, say, "Wouldn't it be Luverly" from *My Fair Lady.* A patter song by Gilbert and Sullivan, like "I am the Very Model of a Modern Major General," expects a different-sounding English from Cole Porter's "Night and Day." This may appear obvious, but I have witnessed many a disastrous attempt at crossover singing when the disaster was perpetuated by the way the singer articulated the text. It is certainly worth carefully considering the source and style of the words, as well as the music.

- *Do not overexaggerate the articulation of the words.* Clarity is essential and how you form words for singing may feel sometimes like an exaggeration but be careful not to go too far. Your audience should be paying attention to *what* you are saying, not *how* you are saying it. The aim is to communicate clearly and be understood, and for this we need, in Patsy Rodenburg's words, "economy, efficiency, and effortlessness." The articulation itself must remain unremarked and invisible; doing its job but not calling attention to itself.

When it comes to words, then, your task as a singer is to make sure you are communicating clearly and honestly with the listener. Every word we shape is part of our commitment.

COMMITMENT IN PRACTICE

Singers are usually told that unlike certain other musicians like pianists, violinists, and flutists, it could actually be unhealthy for us to practice for too long. (It is of course unhealthy for any of these musicians to practice *too* long, but the limit is much higher.) Not for us the twelve hours a day of slogging away to perfect a piece; the vocal mechanism is way too delicate to take such abuse. If we tried such a thing, we would surely end up hoarse or voiceless for several days, however healthy our technique. We have to be careful not to overuse our voices, especially if we haven't yet figured out the correct way to use them!

But for many singers this can mean shirking on commitment and allowing themselves to be lazy. A friend of mine who ended up as a professional singer told me that when he was young he had been an excellent pianist, but one day someone commented that he also had a lovely voice. His choice to pursue singing rather than the piano was purely because he discovered you didn't have to practice half so much! With this book I am emphasizing that singing is not only about using our voices but also involves a complex and intricate connection to every part of ourselves. So we can "practice" singing without singing. Breathing and articulation exercises, muscle strengthening, aerobic exercise, meditation, focusing exercises, memorization, learning a new melody, language studies, even reading books about your craft, or focused listening to other singers are all beneficial components of a singing workout. So if you are vocally tired it doesn't mean you can't go on working at making yourself the best singer you can be. The committed singer—the one who will be successful—knows this.

Not only do you have to commit yourself to practicing regularly, you also have to be committed *when* you practice. This means that the short bursts of practice you do are far more productive. I have had many students who, when I ask them how much singing they have done since their last lesson, respond with, "Oh, I've been singing along with the radio all week!" or "I sing to myself in the car because my family doesn't like it when I sing at home." I quickly remind them that they will never change bad habits if they are not practicing *consciously*.

All the old habits will pop right back unless your mind and body are fully committed to changing the things that have been going wrong, and that means *doing things differently from the past.* It takes conscious effort to do that and so, especially in the beginning of one's learning path, you should never practice while distracted by other things. It is not practice if you do; it is merely repetition. (If Albert Einstein was correct and insanity is doing the same thing over and over again and expecting different results, then there are a lot of crazy singers around!)

Remember that practice is also a time to discover how you feel about a particular song. You must not only commit to technique while practicing but also to familiarizing yourself with your emotional responses. Occasionally students will tell me that they can only fully commit themselves to performing a song when they are actually on a stage in front of an audience. They don't feel comfortable doing it in the studio or in practice. My response to them is that if you don't warn your body what it might go through when you do fully commit yourself *before* you get out in front of people, you may be in for a nasty surprise. Emotionally charged breath works differently from calm breath, and you may not be able to get through those phrases. Or, on the other hand, you may surprise yourself in practice when you add that extra dimension and discover that a particular piece actually becomes easier to sing. It is very important to sing all the time from your authentic center and be completely committed to that center. That way you discover the singer you really are and become familiar with, and in control of, that singer before it has a chance to surprise you and possibly knock you off balance in performance.

That is not to say, of course, that you have to sing *loudly* all the time. Loud does not equal authentic or committed. What we must do is commit ourselves to exactly what we need to be doing to fully express the song—maybe soft, maybe loud, maybe clear, or maybe breathy—and we must do that *in practice* to ever expect to find any sort of consistency in performance.

I should mention here that there are times in rehearsal for opera or shows when it is *advisable* to sing only half voice or take high phrases an octave lower—what is called *marking* in the business. This avoids overexertion of the vocal mechanism when rehearsals are long with much repetition for the sake of staging. But marking itself is dangerous if not done in the right way, i.e., fully on the breath and still with a connection to your center. You must keep your body attuned to the exertion level needed for a particular role (laziness is never an option!), or the voice will become strained from lack of support if it doesn't get it. Once again, commitment is the key.

COMMITMENT IN PERFORMANCE

Many times you will notice less than full commitment in performance by the little things that go wrong: slips of memory (from not truly committing yourself to learning), problems with technique (from falling back into those old habits and not committing yourself to applying your new technique to your performance), or an inattentive audience (who is not engaged because you don't commit yourself to communicating the text or your feelings with them and sharing the song and yourself completely). Obviously we have to commit ourselves fully when in performance, but it is sometimes the most difficult time to do so, since full commitment in front of an audience is hampered by our natural fight-or-flight instinct.

When we are about to perform we are usually nervous, anxious, and fearful—all states that cause a physical response rooted in the days when mankind had to face a foe and fight or run away as quickly as possible. We experience butterflies in the pit of our stomachs, a racing heart, and a dry mouth. So even if your mind is telling you to fully commit yourself to doing this performance, your body is expressing doubts and saying it might be a better idea to get out of there! All sorts of physical tensions can arise, as well as a real ambivalence that hinders our belief in ourselves and therefore prevents complete commitment.

I can only say that aside from addressing the physical and mental issues (chapter 7 and chapter 4), simply focusing on commitment to your singing will help your nerves. Constantly remind yourself that you are there to *give* something special to your listeners, not to *take* praise or adoration, so the song and your means of conveying it (the emotional and technical use of your voice) are what you focus on. You commit yourself to the giving and forget the taking. (I will come back to this in chapter 9.)

TESTING THE WATER

The problem we have as singers is that we want to hear our voices first before we fully commit ourselves. We want to "test the water", so we have an opportunity to withdraw should we judge ourselves not good enough. Of course this leads to doing the very thing that makes that judgment inevitable—we only half-sing. We don't commit enough breath, so other ineffective mechanisms attempt to take over the job of support; we don't commit our bodies, so our singing lacks energy or connection; and we don't commit our emotions or our thoughts about the song, so all communication is impeded. Only a shadow of our full potential is left, and inevitably we judge ourselves to be no good! So the cycle goes on.

What we must learn to do instead of testing the water is to jump in, to take the risks, and trust the outcome.

Trust and Risk

I have to add here that total commitment can be present not only in the things that go *right*, but also in the little things that go *wrong*. In other words, commitment does not guarantee success.

I once heard a trumpet player playing a virtuoso piece with a particularly difficult high note at the very end. Afterward, an interviewer asked if it was scary to have to end the piece like that and didn't it take a lot of guts to do it. The trumpeter said that playing any music was not for the fainthearted. Yes, it was nerve-racking, but all he could do was go for it 100 percent and hope for the best. Less than that and he was *bound* to fail; by giving his all, at least there was a chance that it would work. That day it did, but there had been times when it didn't. That young man had learned to trust to the moment and take the risk. He trusted enough to risk and risked trusting. That indeed is the path to success.

What we must resist doing is equating our *effort* with failure, should that happen. It is never going to be commitment that *creates* the problem. The important thing is to be aware enough (that is, conscious enough) to pinpoint what is the culprit for the cracked note. Muscular tension in the wrong place or a thought that we may not make it just as we come to the difficult note or many other potential hazards we throw up in our own way all can result in difficulties and possible failure.

I have heard many very committed singers make mistakes or fluff notes. Once, at a performance of Verdi's *Rigoletto* by a highly regarded, professional opera company, I heard the lead tenor crack the high note at the end of the famous aria "La Donna e Mobile." Not to be deterred, he walked down to the front of the stage, attempted the ending twice more *a capella*, cracking the high note each time, shrugged, and walked off stage. At least he provided good entertainment and excellent gossip for the intermission!

Full commitment doesn't always lead to success on a plate, but I would like to propose that less than that *never* does, especially in the realm of our own satisfaction and our quest to be the best singer we can be.

THE MYTH OF PERFECTION

We learn, then, that perfection in singing is an elusive concept and not very productive if we think of it in terms of never making mistakes, always sounding just right, or just the same. It could be said that perfection in the way most people understand it is impossible as a reality in the singer's world. Our simple humanity and the nature of singing as the conduit of expression of that humanity means that our singing will always be in some way "flawed" or "imperfect." What a freeing thought that is!

Or, to look at it differently, maybe we singers need to redefine the idea of perfection and simply decide that whoever we are and wherever we are on our journey, we are already perfect. Always perfect and always changing. When you accept that, you free yourself to be where you are, free the song itself, and sharing your authentic voice becomes the only thing that matters. Now you can be completely comfortable to take the committed risks that will open up a world of possibilities and allow yourself the opportunity to understand what commitment really is.

DISCOVERING THE HUMILITY OF COMMITMENT

Finally, one thing to remind ourselves is that commitment is humble. We could so easily shirk our duty to full immersion in our singing and be tempted to gloss over the important details if we think we already know everything we need to know. To fully commit, we must take the ego out of the process and always be looking to learn more. As I said in the introduction, we are never at the end of our singing journey. We never stop learning new things, so commit to looking for the extra detail in the music or the next revelation in your technique, and you will be surprised and delighted by what your commitment uncovers.

PRACTICING COMMITMENT:

Practicing your commitment in the context of singing is as much as anything about awareness. In chapter 4 we will delve into the areas of focus and concentration that will aid this awareness that is at the core of commitment. Remind yourself to stay conscious of what you are doing and above all *be honest* with yourself about how and whether you are truly committing yourself. The questions that follow will help you discover the truth about yourself and point you in the direction of full commitment. Take time to write down responses, either now or as you notice things in your singing:

- *Identify your fears.* They may be general ("I'm afraid I'll make a fool of myself") or specific ("I'm afraid I will run out of air at this phrase"). What would it take to eliminate the fear? (Self-confidence, technical work, etc).

- *Determine what prevents you from taking the necessary steps to address those fears.* Is laziness or ambivalence in the way? Ask yourself the tough questions and be honest. Admit your weaknesses.

- *Decide what you want to commit to.* Do you want to go for broke and head for stardom? Or do you just want to enjoy singing in a choir or karaoke for fun? The commitment necessary to be the singer you want to be in any of these contexts is the same, since we are simply always committing ourselves to do what we need to do fully for the goal we have in mind. But letting go of your own expectation of perfection as a soloist, when that is not where you are headed, can be very freeing. Be committed to being the singer *you want to be*, not the singer you think you *should* be.

- *Think about what happens to you in performance.* What are you thinking about just before you go on stage? Are you focused on the right thing—the song/role not yourself? Do you dare to take technical risks or do you hold back? Write down how you would like to feel when you get on stage. Imagine yourself singing wonderfully, exactly the way you would like it to be. Create a list of the positive aspects of your best performance.

- *List the things in your voice you want to change or improve.* Are your dissatisfactions general or specific? Technical or emotional? Focus on making one improvement at a time. Discuss your goals and your technical problems with your teacher. Don't make her guess where you would like to go with your singing or what problems you feel you need to address.

- *Pay attention to detail.* Are you doing the things suggested by your teacher in every aspect? Are you remembering posture, breath, vowel formation, etc.? Have you studied the text? Do you have a clear idea of what you want to say through this song? Have you thought carefully about what the composer/lyricist is trying to say? Speak the words aloud as a monologue, paying attention to the emphasis and phrasing, and explore the words separately from the music. Write down all your ideas about the song in detail.

- *Delve deeper into your approach to the technical and emotional aspects.* When you do fully commit to a song, is it uncomfortable in some way? Do you need to fix a technical problem? Do your emotions get in the way? Are you addressing these problems or just hoping they will go away? Once again, look in detail, be honest with yourself, and take the necessary steps.

- *Stay aware of your commitment to communicating the message of your song through the words.* We can become so familiar with the text of our songs that we forget that the audience may be hearing it for the first time. Ask yourself if someone who has never heard this song before would understand what the words are trying to express. The physical and mental energy it takes to ensure the listener's understanding of what you are trying to say may take you by surprise. Don't underestimate the hard work you have to commit to when it comes to clear communication.

- *Stay committed to the whole.* Notice that when you commit yourself to one aspect, all others seem to be affected. If you energize your articulation, your breath suddenly may work better; if you pay attention to fully committing to the breath, your performance begins to come alive; and if you immerse yourself in the song emotionally, all of a sudden you find your words become clearer and your communication is enhanced. There is a connection between all elements of singing: realize that shirking on any part will detrimentally affect on the whole.

- In the end, to quote the famous commercial tagline, "*just do it.*" The energy of commitment is one of the most important factors in the emergence of the great singer. Don't pretend to do it, don't do it halfway, and don't try to do it. Just do it.

Make a commitment to commitment!

CHAPTER 4

MIND OVER CHATTER

TAKING CONTROL OF YOUR THOUGHTS

*"The brain gives the heart its sight. The heart
gives the brain its vision"*
– Rob Kall
"'Tis the mind that makes the body rich"
– William Shakespeare

Students are often stumped when I ask "What is the most important organ in the body for singing?" Some will say the larynx, some the diaphragm, some the vocal chords, but few give me the answer I'm looking for—the brain. A light bulb goes on when I say it, and they usually laugh or act like it was a trick question. But I ask it because few people think about singing that way; singing happens in the body, so that is what they focus on. Everyone will agree that the brain is ultimately in control, but they will say that it's something outside of the really important things like having enough air, finding resonance, loosening the jaw, or whatever problem they're experiencing that week. My assertion is that to take control of our thoughts is to take control of the very roots of our problems and thus give ourselves a chance to solve them.

THE MIND OF A SINGER

"A state of consciousness is characteristically very transitory; an idea that is conscious now is no longer a moment later."
– Sigmund Freud

How conscious are you when you sing? Take a moment to imagine yourself singing either in rehearsal or in a voice lesson or in performance. What is going on in your head? In each or any circumstance are you consciously aware of fully connecting to the song, attending to technical issues, directing your breath, feeling the vibrations, or experiencing and communicating the emotions? Or are you wondering what other people (your friend in the next room, your colleague in the choir, your voice teacher, or the audience) think of you? Are you waiting for your teacher to tell you what you did wrong and give you the magic formula to fix it? Or are you remembering what happened last time you tried to sing this song and panicking because a particularly difficult passage is coming up? In other words, are you consciously *in the moment* of singing or does your mind take you somewhere else? It happens to us all—our thoughts wander away from what we are doing without our even noticing. But staying aware while we are singing and focusing on the task at hand is the key to success; it is the only way we learn while practicing or in a voice lesson and the only way we fulfill our goal of a successful performance.

So what do we have to do to take control of our mind?

RECOGNIZING THE TWO VOICES

We live our lives with two internal voices constantly nagging us that seem to influence and direct almost every aspect of our lives. To take control of our thoughts, and, therefore, of our singing, we need to understand and address these two characters.

The first voice I call the *Controller*. This is the loud voice of our ego that begins to develop in childhood and by the time we are teenagers usually dominates. It is the voice that admonishes us to fit in, to please others, to look and sound good and not make fools of ourselves. Or, conversely, it may tell us to challenge society, break the rules, and deliberately prompt a negative response from the outside world. It is that *response* that matters. The Controller is concerned with others' opinions because its aim is to attract as much attention as it can. Attention is how it gets fed, the way it becomes strong, and the way it feels valued. This is also the voice of our own personal judge who sits on the outside, watching and passing judgment on our every move (more of him in chapter 5). It tells us we *should* be doing *this* (earning a lot of money, getting good grades, eating less, and practicing more) or *shouldn't* be doing *that* (reading a book when there's work to be done, smoking that cigarette, being too emotional, or laughing at that inappropriate joke). Very soon we're surrounded by a wall of "shoulds" (or "shouldn'ts"), and a loud voice of ego that screams self-judgment and directs our every move. It is so loud it invariably muffles our second, very quiet voice.

This second voice I call the *Adviser,* and it is the voice of our authentic self, of our very souls. It is the voice that tells us what we really want, what we need, what is right for us, and not what we *should* be doing. It may guide us to do lots of good things for others—in fact it probably will. It will do this not for the sake of our ego image, but because it's right for us or simply the right thing to do. You might call this the voice of intuition or inner guide or sixth sense; in some cultures it might be considered a manifestation of the Tao, the Higher Self, or chi. You could indeed call it the voice of our humanity because it is a voice we have in common with everyone else; it connects us to other people and for this reason is most likely to be concerned with everyone's well-being and not just our own. For some people it is a very clear voice and for some it is almost inaudible. But even if we hear it, we tend to be very reluctant to pay attention to it and are apt to shut it out from our consciousness. What few realize is that this is the voice that leads us to our happiness. It will tell us what is morally and ethically right for us and what we need for our own fulfillment, as well as what is best for the world. It will tell us the truth in all circumstances.

This is not necessarily some mystical thing or out-of-body experience. It is the voice that will come screaming out at times of great urgency and potential disaster. There are numerous stories of heroic deeds when people exhibit extraordinary bravery and afterward express how they were impelled to do what they did not necessarily by courage (at least consciously) but by necessity. They were guided to act by their inner voice, their Adviser. It is the voice that comes out (quite literally) when we see a child about to step out in front of a moving car; without worrying about what we will sound like or how we will look, we do and/or scream whatever is necessary to avert the potential disaster.

So why, you might ask, do we ignore this inner voice so often when it seems to have our best interests at heart? Partly it is because we usually cannot conjure up the Adviser by striving or forcing. We have to stop, shut out the loud, raucous voice of the Controller and simply listen—something that has become increasingly difficult to do in this noisy, hectic, ego-nurturing world. We live in a *world* of Controllers who tell us that if we want approval or love or power, we have to do it their way. In this ego-dominated world success is measured by how much we please these demanding judges. Of course what we don't realize in the beginning of our undertaking to please is that there is *no pleasing them*. The judges will always judge and the egos, including our own, will never be satisfied.

Right Brain and Left Brain

Another reason we have a tendency to ignore the Adviser involves the makeup of our brains. In her fascinating and enlightening book *My Stroke of Insight*, Jill Bolte Taylor, herself a Harvard-trained brain scientist, tells us of her experience after suffering a massive stroke, which effectively cut off access to her brain's left hemisphere. One of the first things she noticed was that the chattering voice of self-talk and self-judgment disappeared, silenced by the trauma. She realized that living in her right brain, though she had lost many functions and most of her memory, gave her a very peaceful, euphoric feeling. She also discovered a sense of oneness with the world because she had lost her sense of physical boundaries. The story of her journey back to health is remarkable, and she emphasizes that to fully function in the world, we need both sides of our brain. But left-brain dominance is the norm, which, according to Taylor, means dominance of that loud chattering ego-voice. The right brain has a remarkable ability to focus on the present, to be compassionate and nonjudgmental, but it is so often subordinated to our self-consciousness. So the voices of the Controller and the Adviser seem to be the battling voices of the two sides of our brain, and the Controller, for the most part, seems to be winning.

To listen to and hear our Adviser, then, we must find a way to develop our right-brain function. (I will address this later in the chapter.) But we also have to face our deep-rooted fear of changing what is familiar and safe to us and to everyone who knows us. Fear is very adept at making us deaf to our own needs and desires.

SINGING AND THE ADVISER

I only slowly became aware of my Adviser, and it was through my singing that I discovered it. After years of taking voice lessons and singing less than satisfactory performances, I came to a crossroads in my singing journey. I knew I had to choose between giving up completely and changing something.

I was in the middle of a concert of opera excerpts, and I was singing a difficult duet with a colleague. I was almost at the end and a string of high notes was bringing us to the climax of the piece. Suddenly I felt my throat closing up as if I were being strangled; it was a sensation I'd never been aware of before. My mind told me I was not going to be able to reach the notes. The first high G came out reluctantly, but there were about three more in the phrase to follow and a long held one at the end. I squeezed out those notes, in grim determination to keep them on pitch, but the sound was not the free voice I had been used to in practice. Having been told all my life what a lovely, *beautiful* voice I had, I was devastated that I could make such sounds. In the months that followed that awful experience, I felt the same strangling hands around my throat on many occasions as I tried singing high notes that once had been no problem. Something had to change if I were to carry on singing.

Then I started to listen to my Adviser. The first thing it told me clearly was that I needed to keep singing. Whenever I thought of giving up singing and lived with that idea for a week or two, I found myself feeling as though a part of me had died. I had to sing to feel whole. It was part of who I was. Clearly I couldn't give up. So how was I to transform myself into the singer I wanted to be? Hadn't I been trying to change things for years? I'd certainly been working hard, practicing regularly, and doing what I thought were all the right things for success. I meditated on the idea of changing for a while, and it came to me that I'd been hearing my inner voice talk to me for years and simply ignored it. "You know that doesn't feel really comfortable" it would say when I approached a high note in the wrong way or tried to force a note into the wrong place because it saved me air. "You know that doesn't sound as beautiful as it should" I heard when I wasn't freeing my breath to find the perfect resonance for the pitch and forcing from my throat once too often. I usually wasn't even aware of the tensions and problems I was creating, but I certainly knew it didn't feel right. And the strange thing was, most of my teachers in one way or another were telling me exactly the same thing all along, but I just was not ready to hear it because I wasn't ready to let go of my beloved, *safe* habits. Then came the crisis, my crossroads, and the need for something to change.

When the student is ready, the teacher will appear goes the saying. In my case, that teacher ended up being my own inner voice, my Adviser; all of a sudden I could hear it because I gave up my desperate fear of changing. As soon as I allowed the Adviser to guide my singing, I suddenly realized it spoke to me in every aspect of my life. Once again, I'm not talking about "hearing voices." I'm talking about getting in touch with an inner part of myself, my authentic self, and discovering how wise it was when I really listened!

HEARING THE VOICE OF YOUR ADVISER

So how do you hear this voice? First, become aware that it is there and give yourself a chance to listen. Understand that one reason we don't listen to it often is that what it has to say is often at odds with what our Controller, the ego, wants—approval and safety. So you have to drop the defense and jump into risky territory.

- You might want to take a moment to reflect on what your Adviser might be saying to you right now. It will talk to you very candidly about how you feel about things, if you really listen. It will tell you what you want, what you need, and what you have to do. They may be things you don't want to hear. But open your mind and ears to it and see. You still have a choice in the end. Just listen for a while.

- Apply your listening particularly to your singing. What is it about your singing you don't like? What would you like to improve? What would you like to feel? Write down everything you can think of that is not as you would like it to be in your voice. Start with the very general: *I'd like my voice to feel freer. I wish my breath would flow more evenly. I'd like my voice to be warmer. I'd like to have a bigger range.* Then be more specific: *I'd like to be able to sing a high C. I'd like my register change to be smoother. I'd like my middle voice to have more focus. I'd like my B-C-C# not to disappear down my throat!* Don't simply write *I want my voice to sound like Ella Fitzgerald's* because your voice is not hers and will only tie itself in knots trying to be. Always remember, your voice is unique and that uniqueness is what will make people love it! What we are after here is to discover your voice and free it. Only then will it be able to express your own unique understanding and experience of the music, the words, and life.

- Now take a look at your list. Do you already know how to fix those problems? Think about the feeling you get when you sing a note that isn't comfortable. Where is the discomfort? Why not stop tightening your throat or the particular muscles that feel uncomfortable and use your breath and body instead, as your teacher has always taught you? Why don't you? Because it doesn't sound strong? Because all of a sudden you feel out of control? Why is that? Maybe the muscles you *need* to be using are lazy or weak or you haven't spent enough time letting go of control to allow your breath to find its way to the fullest resonance. But you already know that instinctively, don't you? It's just too scary to give up your old habits because you don't know right now what will replace them because you haven't experienced it yet! How can you have? Your practice here is honesty. Be truthful with yourself. Don't let your Controller dominate. Stop judging your result and stop working *too hard* to fix things. Just listen to your instincts and pay attention.

So now you've looked the fear right in the eye. Are you going to give up torturing yourself and follow your Adviser? You may need to give yourself lots of time and have lots of patience to create new habits, strengthen what needs to be strengthened, and begin to trust where your inner voice (your right brain) takes you. Even with the acknowledgement of your problems and listening carefully to your Adviser, things won't change overnight. The Adviser is, after all, your guide and not your rescuer. But I assure you it's worth it in the end. After I started to trust my Adviser, it took some time and a lot of hard work, but I found the freedom I was looking for.

I believe you can help develop the vital awareness of the voice of your Adviser by adding another practice to your daily singing routine.

MEDITATION

I have become a great advocate of meditation for singers. Meditation is slowly becoming a more common practice in Western culture, and proponents of its benefits and practitioners are certainly growing in number, though it remains mysterious to many. I know when I was first introduced to the term many years ago, it conjured up images of white-robed, gray-haired gurus sitting cross-legged in a sort of trance, obviously achieving a state I could never dream of reaching. Usually coupled then with the colorful word *transcendental,* it had a sort of magic about it.

But I discovered that meditation is not magical, though what it can bring about certainly can feel that way. It is through meditation that we can begin to calm our demon Controller and allow ourselves access to the quiet Adviser, the inner voice of our true selves. So meditation is, it seems to me, the best way to encourage the development of the right brain. By doing so, it also helps us align our thoughts and focus our energies on the present moment; for a singer that means on our singing, our song, and our emotional response.

Our fear of failure, fear of exposure, fear of judgment, and fear of not meeting expectations are all products of our thoughts. Meditation not only helps us take control of those negative thoughts to enable us to focus on the positive, but it also has the power to guide us to our fears and help us face them, enabling us then perhaps not to conquer them, but to put them into the background so their influence is greatly weakened, as the more important aspects of the purpose of our singing come to the fore.

As well as profoundly affecting brain function, meditation can also help the singer release physical tension by encouraging relaxation of muscles that in our singing only take away energy from the task at hand. It is also a perfect chance for allowing creative inspiration and finding a deeper connection to a particular song, as I'll discuss later in chapter 8.

Practicing Meditation

You may be saying to yourself, "I don't need to meditate to take control of my thoughts, I'm quite in control, thank you!" Begin to notice how many times a day you find yourself doing one thing while your mind is somewhere else. Become aware of the path your mind takes while you are in a conversation or watching television or doing your work or driving down the road. Pay attention to what your mind is thinking about while you are practicing singing or just singing around the house. In other words, become *fully* conscious. You will probably discover what the Buddhists call your *monkey mind*, leaping from thought to thought like a monkey in the trees. We all do it. It is in the nature of the mind to lead us away to other places, harkening back to experiences of the past or leaping to future possibilities or scenarios. But by doing so, our minds prevent us from devoting vital energy to the present moment. And without complete attention in the moment, accidents happen or we miss important signs, or we fail to experience an essential lesson.

People say, "I can't meditate. I've tried, and I can't do it." But I contend that meditation is not in fact something that you can be

judged as able to do or not; you simply have to have patience with
yourself and leave your expectations at the door. It definitely gets
easier with practice, but meditation is in its essence a very simple
thing to begin if you just make the decision to do it (and commit
to it!). I would venture to say that the person who gives up on it
the quickest needs it the most! If you cannot sit down with yourself and be quiet for ten or twenty minutes and pay attention to
your thoughts, you are probably burying a lot of problems that
you are afraid to face. So give yourself a chance and do it now.
If you find yourself wanting to get up and run from it after a few
minutes, try again tomorrow. Here's how to begin:

- Sit comfortably either cross-legged on a cushion or seated
  on a chair and ensure that your spine is strong and straight.
  You may touch your fingers together in front of you or
  hold your hands comfortably out to the side, resting them
  on the cushion or your knees, with your palms up. Close
  your eyes. Keep your mouth closed but relax your jaw and
  let your tongue touch the roof of your mouth.

- Now breathe deeply through your nose and out through
  your mouth so you hear your breath move. Concentrate
  on your breath. IN...OUT...IN...OUT. Visualize it moving
  in and out of your body. Follow its path. Stay focused on
  your breath for a while. If you notice your mind wandering
  and find yourself thinking of other things, just acknowledge it and bring your thoughts back to your breath. You
  will probably have to do this frequently at first, but that's
  fine. Just silence that voice telling you you're no good at
  this and keep repeating the process. Don't run away. It
  gets easier. Breathe...notice your thoughts...come back to
  the sensation of the breath.

- After a while you can bring your thoughts to your hands.
  Observe how they feel. If they are touching each other,
  imagine energy passing between them. Imagine your
  breath flowing into your hands and see if you can make
  them warmer or make them tingle. If they are resting on
  a cushion, pay attention to what they are touching. How

does it feel? Do this with any or every part of your body. Your neck, for instance. Notice what it's doing, and what it feels like. If there's tension, try to breathe into it, and let it go. If there's pain, notice it, pay it some attention, and try to let that go, too. Or not. This is more an exercise in awareness than a cure. You are using your breath as a focal point to keep you here and now, not somewhere in the future.

- Now become an observer of yourself. In your mind's eye, see yourself as you are now, sitting and breathing. How do you look? Can you clearly see your own face? This can now become an exercise in strength of imagination, something vitally important for a great singer. Make the image as detailed as you can. If you lose it come back to the breath and start again. Make the image appear again on the screen of your imagination. The important thing is to not leave this moment and stay conscious of where you are and what you are doing right now.

- You may want to use a mantra to find your focus. A mantra can be any short phrase that you say over and over again to yourself to keep your attention from wandering elsewhere. Find a two- or three-word mantra that will work for you— something calming and perhaps affirming. Choose something simple in your own language (e.g., Let...go..; Be...peace; Calm...breath; or, simply, In...Out...) or find traditional suggestions of phrases in Sanskrit from a meditation book that may save you from being distracted by the words' literal meaning. So'ham [I am that] is a traditional one.

The act of meditating is known as practicing, which is exactly what you need to do regularly to make a difference and enjoy the benefits. Begin with just five minutes. Add a minute a day if you can. As you get more comfortable with it, go to ten, twenty, then thirty minutes. Always begin by spending as much time as you need to focus your attention on the breath; don't move on to the second stage until you feel relaxed and focused. You may stay with the breath the whole time. If you are interested in taking meditation further, seek out a meditation class or pick up some books on meditation; there are many good ones to be found.

I will be presenting more ideas and exercises for meditation in later chapters, but begin with the simple, though not to say easy, task of noticing the breath, and then channeling thoughts. Meditation is like a workout for the brain. It puts us on the path to controlling our monkey minds. To uncover the singer you want to be, it can be invaluable.

Flow: A Step Toward Happiness

"We cannot reach happiness by consciously searching for it…It is a circuitous path that begins with achieving control over the contents of our consciousness."
– Mihaly Csikszentmihaly, *Flow*

In his thought-provoking book *Flow: The Psychology of Optimal Experience*, Mihaly Csikszentmihaly describes that wondrous state of concentration experienced by us all at one time or another when we are so focused on one particular task, that time seems to stand still and all the rest of life fades into the background. It may happen while we are playing chess, running, walking in the woods, reading a book, making love, eating a favorite meal, or working on an important project; the moment will be different for everyone. It may well involve great physical or mental effort and certainly intense concentration. But, according to the author, these experiences will be the closest we will ever come to true happiness. He calls this state *flow.* It is true present moment immersion. He points out that it also involves "a loss of self-consciousness, which does not mean a loss of self, and certainly not a loss of consciousness, but rather, only *a loss of consciousness of self.*" In other words, it encourages a loss of ego in favor of the emergence of the true self. Goodbye, Diva; hello, Authentic Singer.

Singing seems to me to have perfect *flow* potential (and therefore, according to Csikszentmihaly, perfect happiness potential). It offers us moments of full connection to ourselves through the symbiosis of breath, body, and mind, while allowing us to connect to others, i.e., the composer, the poet, and the listeners. Ideally it keeps us rooted in the present, and yet offers us glimpses of the past (the song itself) and may influence the future (the effect of change in ourselves or our audience). When we sing, time feels as if it stands still while we immerse ourselves in another world, another's mind, or our own bodily experiences of free vibrations and engulfing emotions. If we allow *flow* into our singing, it is at this point that we can become truly great, allowing a powerful emergence of our authentic self, unflinching in its courage to share our own experiences and feelings with others, as the *flow* of the moment distracts us from our fears. Finding the tool to conquer those fears makes *flow* valuable indeed!

THE *FLOW* EXPERIENCE

To better understand *flow*, pick up an interesting book and begin to read a few pages. If it really interests you, after a few minutes' immersion, nothing except the loudest interruption can disturb you from its pages. If other thoughts intrude as you read the words, you will have to reread passages where your mind has strayed. Even if the radio or television is on while you are reading, you will have to divert your attention to those things to even register them because your brain cannot do two things at once. (If you do multitask, tests have proven that you have to effectively throw your mind rapidly back and forth from one thing to another; no wonder certain countries and states have laws against using a cell phone while driving!)

When we read like that we aren't aware of how we look, what other people are thinking of us, what the results of our action might be. We simply read. *Flow* is easily attained because no one else involved. The ego is submerged. The same is true for the mountain climber or sportsman whose concentration is on only the task at hand. It is with the introduction of a second party to the activity that self-consciousness threatens to take over again, hindering complete focus (*flow*) and thus, according to Csikszentmihaly, hindering our path to complete happiness, satisfaction and success.

Now think of singing. To immerse ourselves in *flow* whilst singing we have to be as focused on the act of singing and the world of the particular song, just as we might be in the world of the stories we read. But there are two possible distractions: the judgment of an outside listener and that of our own inner judge (More about this in chapter 5.) Since it is very difficult to completely eliminate these distractions, the solution is to relegate them to the periphery by intense concentration on what I call the Singer's Gift. This is the total package of the performance: the music, poetry, experience, and emotion (the right brain's job), along with the vocal technique required to convey it (the left brain's contribution).

Flow and the focus that implies can then work wonders in our singing by distracting us from the pesky ego voice that is so quick to judge and by making us aware of things we need to be paying attention to. Our focus is on the act of singing and on the song itself, so fears, nervousness, and self-consciousness dissolve.

Steps to Finding *Flow*:

- *Use your experience with meditation techniques to apply to your singing practice.* Pick a topic in your practice and focus on just that. For instance, you can start with the breath. Pay close attention as you sing a particular song to what the breath does, how and where you breathe, where you are short of breath, or any other detail concerning the use of breath. Try not to think of or notice anything else. Then take the words. Think about your formation of the vowels, making of the consonants, what your articulators are doing to form the words, and all the details concerning just the shaping of the words themselves. Next look at the emotional content behind the words and the music. Reflect on what you are feeling at a specific moment in the song. Consider the meaning of and your emotional response to each sentence or phrase. Take your singing to pieces and focus on one aspect at a time. Try not to be distracted by anything other than what you have decided to focus on. Don't judge, simply observe; this is primarily an exercise in focus, not vocal technique. You may also discover some very interesting things happen in your voice in the process, since in distracting our minds away from certain problems, sometimes they will disappear altogether.

- *Pretend you are in performance.* Practice focusing on what you want to communicate and the energy you need to achieve that. This time allow yourself to slip into *flow* not by taking your singing to pieces but by attending to the big picture—concentrate hard on putting across the meaning and intention of the song. Do not judge the results, but simply focus on getting your message out. Intensify your connection to the song. If you *practice* flow as if singing were a meditation in itself, you may be amazed at how much control over it you can have, and how you can silence or at least put out of mind that nagging voice of self-consciousness!

- *Begin to notice your mind and its response when you practice.* Notice that doubting voice in your head that begins to wonder if anyone is listening or starts judging how it sounds or becoming overly critical. Be aware of bringing yourself back to focus on the song or how your body feels. Remind yourself to stay focused as if you were reading a book and you want to know how it ends, so you don't allow yourself to be distracted.

BELIEVING IN YOUR GIFT

Belief in yourself as a singer is central to your success. By uncovering your Authentic Singer and your Adviser you will begin to be led to greater self-confidence to strengthen that belief. But first ask yourself whether you really believe that someone else wants to hear what you have to say through singing?

Consider our exploration in chapter 1 of singing as a means of connection between people, an expression of empathy and a way to share experiences. If you believe this, then you believe in your Gift, and you must keep reassuring yourself of this.

Believing in yourself as a singer does not mean you have to think you have the greatest voice or that you have worked it all out or that you think you are better than anyone else. It means simply you want to seek connections with other people through singing; you want to share yourself and your experiences through your voice.

If you truly *want to share it,* I contend that someone out there *wants to hear what you have to say,* including your interpretation of someone else's song. If you do it in an honest and authentic way from your very core, from your heart, *you will have a gift others want to receive and that no one else has to offer.* For this reason you must believe in the value of your *self* and what you have to say before you can become the singer you want to be.

This may be leading us into realms of self-esteem and psychology beyond the scope of this book or my expertise, but my reason for reminding you of this is that we encounter the mind once again at the center of a very important issue for singers—self-worth. All I can do here is encourage you to see that whatever you have to say through your singing is worthy and important because it is an expression of your humanity. In the end, singing is no more scary a proposition than an intimate conversation. It takes courage and honesty, but is ultimately rewarding, if you keep your mind focused on your task and banish your Diva instincts!

Determine to take control of your mind.

CHAPTER 5

NO, YOUR HONOR

ELIMINATING THE JUDGE

"Life does not have to be regarded as a game in which scores are kept and somebody wins. If you are too intent on winning, you will never enjoy playing. If you are too obsessed with success, you will forget to live."
— Thomas Merton, *Learning to Live*

"In the measurement world, you set a goal and strive for it. In the universe of possibility, you set the context and let life unfold."
— Rosamund Stone Zander and Ben Zander,
The Art of Possibility

In their inspiring book *The Art of Possibility*, Roz and Ben Zander encourage us to step out of what they call the "measurement world" and leap into a "universe of possibility."

The world we live in is a place where competition is the name of the game. It is the world of comparisons, where we are constantly judging or being judged. Labels are king! In this world, we are constantly striving to have more, be the best, and win the race.

This is happening in every aspect of our lives, but perhaps it is nowhere more conspicuous than on our singing journey, where competition is rife and judgment seemingly unavoidable. Our world is filled with auditions, tryouts, and competitions. When we sing, everyone has an opinion, and we (that is, our egos) give equal weight to every comment. (I have seen professional singers devastated by the negative opinion of a ten-year-old!) Most often we are extreme in our reactions, ecstatic when praised and devastated when criticized. When we practice and have no one else to do the job, we judge ourselves, beating ourselves up or stroking our egos according to how the comparison comes out.

For singers, it is vitally important to rid ourselves of the Judge (who is, of course, simply one manifestation of the Controller) and neutralize the effect of others' judgments.

RECOGNIZING THE JUDGE

Consider these dictionary definitions of the verb *to judge*:

- *to pronounce on the guilt or innocence of;*
- *to condemn;*
- *to be censorious toward;*
- *to pass sentence on.*

I believe that our Judge has a tendency toward condemning and being censorious toward because it is inextricably linked to our ego (our sense of self) and lives very much in the world of measurement. Our ego feeds and grows by its comparison to others whether good or bad. In practice or in performance our Judge is ready to leap out at any moment and pronounce sentence. In fact he's always sitting in the wings waiting for the mistake to happen, and when it does, he will admonish us so loudly ("That was awful! How could you make those noises?") that he will stand in the way of everything positive, becoming the barrier to communication and preventing us from taking risks and bolstering our fears. Progress becomes impossible because the Judge stops us in our tracks with his negativity.

He doesn't confine himself to the bad times either. He will also be there when we are particularly successful, ready to distract once more from our task of learning *why* and *how* our success was achieved with ego-inflating praise ("How wonderful you are! Weren't you great today?").

So the Judge will inhibit our path forward because our reaction to his pronouncement focuses our energy on protecting or feeding our ego, rather than analyzing the questions of how we produced the result we got. He thus denies us the opportunity to look past his judgments, and so prevents us from discovering the roots of our problems or uncovering new possibilities.

FACING YOUR JUDGE IN THE VOICE STUDIO

Voice lessons are meant to guide us to improvement and vocal progress. But the Judge's nagging voice may be standing full on in the way of our learning, and it is important to begin to understand how to recognize and overcome this.

I have many students who have come to me paralyzed by their negative judgment of themselves:

- "My voice is so small."
- "I can't sing that note—it's way too high!"
- "I've such a limited range."
- "I've three different voices."
- "My breathing doesn't work."

All I can say is "Good—then something needs to change, so let's change it." We set to work looking at the problems, and I offer advice as to how to go about fixing them. But what happens? They open their mouths to try something different and out comes their judge again to stop them in their tracks—not giving them a chance and making no allowances, just the sentencing them *guilty*! The students don't even have time to observe what they might be doing wrong, so quickly does the gavel drop! Commitment under such circumstances is virtually impossible.

Even when improvement is made, the negative judgment can be relentless.

I had a sixteen-year-old student who was reluctant to sing in a master class I was holding for my students. She had a lovely voice and was to my mind improving greatly every week. When I asked why she wouldn't sing, she said she hated her voice. "But you are singing so well!" I tried to encourage her. "But I don't sound like you!" she said. My jaw dropped. "You are sixteen. You are not supposed to sound like me. You never will sound like me because you're not me!" She had an idea in her head about what a good singer sounded like and not being that very singer made her worthless for anything. Her judge had pronounced sentence and found her guilty of not being good enough.

It is important to understand that our uniqueness is a valuable and wonderful thing. In fact, in singing, it is an essential part of our success. When we compare ourselves to others, we undervalue that uniqueness and take away one of our greatest strengths. So you think there are thousands of people who sing better than you? How many sing much worse? How many comparisons will you have to make to convince yourself you should stop singing altogether because you don't reach the standard? If we stop the comparisons and just aim for doing our best, improving step by step, we will be far less distracted on our journey, and the singer we want to be will have a chance to emerge.

Unfortunately the Judge is very tenacious and in some cases can even be seductive in his power. Some students have come to me not looking to learn to silence that condemning voice but simply looking for a more authoritative one to engage in battle. Teacher's Judge versus student's Judge, egos battling each other. They want my Judge to convince their Judge that they *are* good enough, after all. They want to think that *their* Judge has got it wrong, and the teacher's authoritative Judge will correct their misguided notion and stroke their fragile egos. These are students who are passive in their learning and submissive to the teacher, as well as to their own Judge. Often they will not address their real problems, only hide behind them or expect someone else to fix them. They are waiting for their teachers to *make* them sing better and are unprepared to really apply themselves to the task of learning. Students who take this attitude do not usually stay long with any one teacher, quickly discovering that teachers are not satisfied to be just cheerleaders and have no magic powers to make everything work with a wave of a wand.

As Alan Watts said, "Climbing the signpost that says New York won't get you anywhere." Voice teachers can only act as signposts to point you in the right direction; the student has to actually take the journey.

So the best way to reap rewards from voice lessons is to find a way to finally silence the nagging, judging voice and hear, without judgment, what needs to be done.

INTRODUCING YOUR AUTHENTIC SINGER TO THE PROCESS

Our core self is strong already and has no need to win the race. Our Authentic Singer wants only to give through singing and does not seek to be better than others or to overshadow the competition or to receive all the accolades. It wants to do its best to make singing more pleasurable, more honest, and more valuable to the listener. It wants to improve because improvement leads not only to this goal but also to new and exciting steps along the path. Wouldn't that be far easier and much more satisfying than facing the Judge every day?

So let us take the Zanders' advice and change our approach here. What does a leap into a "universe of possibility" look like in this context?

LEARNING TO DISCERN

The problem can be that we delude ourselves into thinking that the Judge is a valuable, necessary part of our journey. After all, if we don't judge ourselves, how will we improve?

But maybe we could look at it from a different angle and side step the roadblock the Judge erects. Instead of thinking of judging why don't we learn to *discern*?

Discern is defined:

- *to make out, distinguish, by eye or ear;*
- *to determine by acute observation.*

Let us decide not to *judge* ourselves better or worse but simply *discern* that we are where we are, and if that is not where we want to be then decide to change things accordingly. In discerning, we open ourselves to hearing and feeling both the good and the bad aspects of our voice without the distracting emotional component that judgment embodies, so we can stand back and simply observe. Then we act on that observation.

Act is an important word here. Just as judgment inhibits and even paralyzes us, discernment frees us to move on, to *do* something to remedy our problems, and to take our next step. When we judge a problem to be difficult, our tendency is to want to hide from it, ignore it, and hope it goes away; when we discern a problem we turn the spotlight on it, study it, and tackle it. Judgment obfuscates and hinders, discernment illuminates, and aids our progress.

Let me clarify further what I see as the differences between judgment and discernment:

- *Judgment* associates things with our "vertical" striving—being at the top of our profession or climbing the ladder. The higher, the better says the Judge. For the singer stardom (a term implying extreme heights) may be the goal (though not for every singer, of course). We have our singing ups and downs, and presumably we will be happy when we are up and depressed when we are down.

- *Discernment* walks a linear path. We discern we are at a certain place along the path, but since no point on the path is good or bad, we don't feel the pressure to be anywhere in particular. We may want to move forward toward new things, but it's fine if we don't. Our "ups and downs" (now "back and forth") are acceptable because they are the present state of things—the place from which we are always working.

- *Judgment* has an emotional element that dominates our response to the point of inhibiting our forward progress. When a student deems his performance bad, the feeling of inadequacy or incompetence dominates his thoughts and prevents clear inquiry as to why things didn't work better.

- *Discernment* allows for a more pragmatic approach. Unencumbered with emotional baggage, the discerner accepts the way things are, steps back, and looks at why things went wrong and what can be done to fix the problem.

- *Judgment* speaks in terms that are personal, implying the value of the person involved. "He sang off pitch today. She is a fantastic singer. You're not good enough to sing that piece." This approach sets up an emotional reaction in the subject (the singer) that puts him on the defensive and inhibits objective response. Judgment is taken very personally, and the ego feels battered.

- *Discernment* on the other hand is generally more impersonal. "That note was a little flat. Her voice has real beauty. This song is a technically very difficult." By discerning, we take the personal out and become the *objective observer*. We are able to move forward because we understand the elements that can be improved without feeling personally attacked. The ego can step aside as the Authentic Singer is given room to express itself.

- *Judgment* is rooted in an idealistic place, a world of "shoulds", where comparisons are king. We are not as good as yesterday, not improving fast enough, or don't have as beautiful a voice as that perfect singer in our imaginations or the successful star we hear on the radio or the singer who always gets chosen to sing the solos in choir. When we judge, we beat ourselves up with expectations rooted in this imaginary world.

- *Discernment* accepts things as they are now and allows us to choose the best path to travel from here. When we discern, we know comparison to others is unhelpful, since we can only be ourselves, though we have a great appreciation of others' talent and achievements. Expectations of the future or longing for the past are not part of our discernment of what is happening *now*.

- *Judgment* has a single focus: the problem. This causes us to be overwhelmed by a negative view of our singing.

- *Discernment* looks at the big picture, so we can still recognize a problem but also stay aware of the positive aspects of our voice. By discerning we clearly see our problems in the context of the whole.

BEING PRESENT

As long as we allow the Judge to dominate our response to our singing, our minds will be distracted from the task at hand. Instead of addressing *what* is going wrong we become obsessed *that* things are going wrong. Our minds cannot relax enough to allow us to see a solution because we are paralyzed by a fear of failure, that is, fear of negative judgment, both from outside listeners and ourselves. So what is happening here? We are looking to a future outcome and making that our focus, when we should be focused on the present, where we can put *flow* to best use. Then if things do go wrong, we are conscious of what happened and have a basis of information from which to fix it; or if things go perfectly well, we'll know what we did or thought to create that outcome. Teachers often find themselves frustrated beyond measure when the student's response to the question "That was great—what did you do?" is "I don't know!" Most will have been so anxious to hear what their Judge has to say, so distracted by that voice, that even when the result is positive, they are not aware of how they got there because they were *absent from the moment.*

Whenever you sing, whether in practice, in the voice studio, or in performance, make the choice to be present.

THE LISTENER'S JUDGE

How we deal with *other people's* Judges can have as profound an influence on our success in singing as our response to our own.

The most familiar Judges we encounter are:

- Our family, friends, colleagues, or audience members.
- Our voice teacher in the studio.
- Audition panels.

Let's look at each group.

The Judge in the Audience

Opinions from audience members or listeners will be forth-coming, and we must be prepared for that. (How nice it would be to persuade the whole world to discern not judge!) It is our job to hear all opinions objectively and strive to distinguish authentic, useful statements from opinions that may be weighted with per-sonal bias. Remember, there are many factors that affect people's opinions that have no relevance to you and your voice whatso-ever. Consider these examples:

- This person hates soprano voices of any sort and so will never express a positive opinion of yours.
- That listener has had a bad day and was not in the mood to enjoy anything.
- This one may have a need to boost his own ego or show off how much he knows by tearing your technique/interpre-tation/value to pieces.
- That person finds all jazz music irritating.
- This family member wants to support you and boost your confidence by telling you how great you were.

In every case, the opinion expressed has nothing whatsoever to do with your performance. It has everything to do with the other person—his personality, personal taste, or simply the mood he is in that day. Also, remember, the listener who loves bluegrass artist Alison Kraus may cringe at hearing opera singer Renee Fleming and vice versa. It's very hard to please all of the people all of the time, when what people like is determined entirely by their own past experience. However well you might sing, you have no influence on that. Though you do, of course, give them a new experience today that may well influence their response in the future; but this is only possible if they have come with an open mind, which is another aspect over which you have no control.

This is not to say all criticism or compliments are worthless. In fact as singers we *need* feedback because what other people hear is often very difficult for us to determine; the audience is the receiver of our Gift and as such has a completely different experience of our performance. Happily, there are people or critics who can be objectively honest and whose motivation is to help you on your journey. I believe that if you listen carefully enough to your own Adviser—and not to your Judge—you will know perfectly well which those voices are. The ability to discern what is useful criticism or praise is something then that you must nurture. Eliminating your own Judge is the first step.

So what, in the end, do you do with all of the feedback in response to your singing? Listen, assimilate, *discern,* and move on. Don't take criticism personally. Act on what is useful for your own improvement and discard the rest.

THE JUDGE IN THE STUDIO

As far as your teacher is concerned, my advice is to always assume that your teacher is speaking from his authentic core and genuinely motivated to help you improve and guide you along your path. Any other assumption would be completely destructive and unproductive. You must hear what the teacher has to say, set ego aside, and not take criticism—or praise—personally. Once again, simply listen attentively, absorb the information, discern the value for you, decide what you need to do, and act accordingly. See the teacher as someone who discerns rather than judges. A good teacher is also working under the assumption that you are doing your best with where you are now and, knowing that, is not in the business of judging but simply assessing, guiding, and leading.

I believe that any teacher of singing has something of his or her own experience to offer everyone that can be valuable. However, everything a teacher says is not necessarily going to work for you, so hanging on every word and obeying instructions like a performing dog is not the way to make the most of your voice lessons. Remind yourself that simply pleasing your teacher, searching only for approval, is an example of attempting to feed your Diva instincts and will lead you nowhere. A teacher can be motivated purely and authentically and *still* suggest things that don't work for *you,* don't feel right, or lead you in a direction you are not comfortable with. The most important thing in voice lessons is *how you feel*, not what your teacher *says is right*. We, the teachers, are not inside your body; we are only the ears and the senses outside. We may have highly developed hearing, sensing, and listening skills, but we are not infallible. It is also worth remembering that your *interpretation* of what your teacher says may be flawed, and you may take something the wrong way or think you are doing what she asks when you are not. So my advice is to *be vigilant*. Try out what your teacher suggests, feel it in your voice, and observe for yourself whether it works. In the end, extracting the value from your lessons is up to you. Like all other aspects of your growth as a singer, you have to work at it.

I'd like to take a moment here to point out another area where negative judgment, rather than discernment, is only destructive. Just as the teacher does not benefit from judging the student harshly, but achieves far more by simply assessing and guiding, so the student wastes vital energy and focus blaming the teacher for his problems and judging the teacher to have failed in her task. If you find no value left in lessons with a particular teacher, by all means find another teacher, but only because you have gained all you can and now need new ears or ideas. Avoid the blame game at all costs. This is where you once again put away your Judge, assess the situation, discern the best path forward, and act on it appropriately. Neither your teacher nor you benefit from your negative judgment of her, so why indulge in it? Of course, if your ego wants an excuse for not doing all it can to create your own success, this is the perfect one: "My voice teacher doesn't know what she's talking about! No wonder I didn't do well in my performance." That is not, however, going to take you any closer to being the singer you want to be. It's a very thorny side path. Better to go back to the main road and just get on with it.

THE JUDGES AT THE AUDITION

The audition panel has its own particular power over us and it seems that we cannot avoid its apparent manifestation as Judge. After all, isn't it their job to judge us in relation to others? But bear in mind that they are only judging you in relation to others for a particular role, a solo, a place in the group, or participation in a performance *in this specific context.* This is still not a judgment on you as a singer as such.

In any case, you have to be aware and honest with yourself about what you did to present the very best audition possible and then discern if you could have done better.

- Did you know the piece as well as you could have?
- Did you sleep enough the night before the audition and have yourself in the best physical shape?
- Did you prepare yourself technically as well as you could have?
- Did you choose the right audition song?
- Were you completely focused on what you were presenting or was your mind distracted by what the panel might be thinking?
- Were you truly singing from your authentic core?
- Did you leave the Diva at the door?

The variations in reasons for lack of success are endless for you and for everyone else who might be auditioning. In the end it simply comes down to what the panel wants that particular day and what vocal or even physical features they are looking for. You either fit those or you don't.

There are some situations where the performers who are auditioning may be completely unsuitable for whatever they are trying out for; we have all cringed at some of the hopefuls singing in the early rounds of *American Idol.* This may be a case of misguided hope or lack of understanding of what training and technique is required to sing at all, let alone pass the audition. To these singers, I say take some lessons and listen to your Adviser before you present yourself if you want to avoid disappointment. Singing may be possible for anyone, but that doesn't mean we all can do it without physical and mental hard work.

It is also possible that there will be times when the outcome of an audition is unjust, perhaps because the panel happened to be working to fulfill their own ego needs or the outcome was in some way predetermined or favoritism was at play. However, none of this has any importance for you because you have no control over it and dwelling on it has no benefit for you whatsoever. Once again, your judgment of the behavior of the audition panel or the performances of the other candidates would only serve to feed and inflate your own ego; it would not take you any further forward on your path. Be careful not to use the story of your lack of success as an excuse for ignoring what you could have done better. Be very honest with yourself about what more you could have done to prepare and determine to do it the next time.

If you indeed know you have prepared as well as you could, sung as well as you could, and still been rejected, the only thing to do is move on. Today you didn't have what the panel wanted, but that does not mean you are worthless. Such self-judgment only hinders your path forward and becomes a specter to haunt future auditions.

Ask any singer who has gone through hundreds of auditions only to be rejected time after time, and she will tell you that you need your energy for the next tryout, and there is no room for self-pity or self-judgment. Your task is simply to discern how to do better next time. Once again, discernment takes the emotion out of your response and allows you to move on.

LISTENING TO OTHER SINGERS

Imagine silencing the Judge also in the context of other singers and your own listening. Instead of judging other singers to be good or bad or great or horrible or whatever word of judgment you might pronounce, begin to simply observe and discern. Without preconceived notions or prejudices stemming from your own ego, you may open yourself to hearing great things in singers who are far from "perfect." Or, on the other hand, you may perceive "imperfections" in singers you have long idolized. Whatever you observe will be purely observations and perceptions though, not judgments. In our new world we are only looking for fresh and greater possibilities and understandings, not condemning or dismissing. By listening without judgment, we free ourselves of expectations.

This doesn't mean to say we have to enjoy every singer we hear. We will still prefer one over another. But we can avoid taking some high road of superiority and learn to appreciate the positive aspects of *anyone's* singing—even if it's just admiration for the bravery to do it at all! If you take the time to listen with an open mind, there are thousands of performers out there singing with their Authentic Voice. Even if the music they sing doesn't instantly speak to you, there is a lot to be learned from their honesty.

If we practice not judging others, we begin to learn to stop judging ourselves. Assuming everyone always does his best, what right do we have to judge anyway?

How Your Best Is Good Enough

If you are performing and have done all the necessary preparation and work on technique required by the demands of the piece you are singing (which means you've begun by doing your best!), *your best will always be good enough.* Your judge can have nothing to say since he could not ask any more of you. The way to silence the Judge is always to do your best, to *understand* that you are doing your best, and to not make excuses.

There is no doubt that there is room for improvement for us all, but that is when we are further along on our journey. Now, in the present moment, we can move toward that improvement by acknowledging that we are doing our best, discerning what we can improve on, and stepping toward it. No judgment, no beating ourselves up, no comparing to what might be or should be or what once was. Just doing our best and moving toward making our best even better the next time!

But what is "your best"?

Your best will never be the same from moment to moment. Your best is determined by numerous factors of circumstance: how you feel physically and emotionally, where you are, what you did yesterday or today, how well suited to your voice the songs you sing are, etc. But doing your best is always possible even taking into account any of these circumstances. The problems arise when we don't believe in our best and give up on full commitment to what we are doing. Commitment yet again is the key.

Too often we begin by making excuses: "I'm so tired/ exhausted/worn out/depressed." Often this simply means "I can't be bothered" or "I don't feel like putting in the effort." Or it could stem from a persistent negative image we project on ourselves and our singing—our negative Judge at work. Or it could be rooted in our fear of failure. Wherever these excuses come from, speaking them aloud or to ourselves will certainly give us the perfect reason to withhold our best. It gives all those mistakes, technical problems, and sense of failure just cause, along with the perfect reason not to address them yet again! Instead of taking responsibility for the outcome, we blame what seems to be out of our control: lack of sleep, a tickle in the throat, bad acoustics, and just about anything but our own lack of commitment.

I would also like to point out here another obstacle some-times in the way of "doing our best." There are some audiences out there who we know will be very forgiving and undemand-ing, who will love everything we do. My students, for instance, sing a recital twice a year for their friends and family. Naturally, it is an audience full of cheerleaders who will love anything the students present. The same could be said for an elderly audi-ence, perhaps in a nursing home, where any entertainment is craved and all appreciated. It is easy in these circumstances for a singer to allow herself to be lazy or not fully committed, feel-ing she can get away with not doing her best and not taking technical or emotional risks. I'm sure it is obvious, however, that this is not a satisfactory approach for your fulfillment and growth or for your audience.

Now imagine how it turns out when you do absolutely every-thing every time to guarantee that you produce your best when-ever you open your mouth to sing. It is never going to be exactly the same each time because the variable, uncontrollable factors involved in your performance are too numerous and too change-able to count. These you learn to accept because they *are* out of your control. What you are always in control of is your involve-ment, your total commitment *at that moment.* In giving that, you will make steps to achieving the consistency and progress your Judge is looking for. Then maybe he'll be quiet for a while.

SEEKING CONSISTENCY

I have always said that to be a successful singer, you have to be "good enough" even on your worst days. Consistency, *within a certain range,* is the only way to stay in the market. Just as a restaurant would soon lose its clientele if its quality fluctuated unpredictably, so the professional singer must adhere to his promise of a certain quality output. The range of acceptable fluctuation for a nonprofessional is of course much greater; often the amateur choral singer, for example, has few demands on his talent apart from staying on pitch and in rhythm, and "success" is determined by a quite different set of markers. (Many, of course, offer and produce much more than that—I make no judgment on choristers!) Whatever your level, your consistency will be determined by doing your best and committing yourself every time.

As I said in chapter 3, in singing there is no such thing as "perfection." At least not as far as those Judges are concerned, that is. But give up your notion of having to be perfect and all of a sudden you are perfect every time because perfection is only related to the moment. If you are doing your best, you are achieving perfection right then and there. Tell that to your Judge next time he steps out to hinder your path!

TAKING RESPONSIBILITY

Having determined to do your best and to stop judging yourself, you must now take the giant leap to taking full responsibility for everything you do.

This means taking responsibility *for your successes and your failures.*

Not judging yourself doesn't mean you won't have failures. It simply means you are not going to beat yourself up for them or label yourself bad, useless, or inferior because of them. But there will be times when things don't go as well as you wished, even though you did your very best. In which case, you may file it away as an unsuccessful performance not a bad you. You will also have successes when you feel really good about a performance, but because you are not judging you will not label *yourself* superior, great, or brilliant, but apply those words only to that particular performance. Of course, each one is *your* performance, so you must take responsibility for it; that includes taking the necessary steps to either improve for the next time or analyze and learn what you did to cause it to go so well. Equanimity is a very useful quality to nurture on our singing path.

Going back to the three singers I talked about earlier, you may recognize that each behaves differently when it comes to this.

- The Diva takes full responsibility for her successes but none for her failures. Her failures are all due to people or circumstances beyond herself. (*The conductor's tempo was far too slow so he ruined my phrasing. The acoustics in the hall were terrible. I didn't sleep well last night. There was something wrong with the sound system. My accompanist wasn't following me.*) What this often means is that she doesn't take steps to fix problems because she won't admit they are there.

- The Introvert blames himself entirely for his failures but rarely even acknowledges his successes. He sees imperfection in everything he does and doesn't give himself a real chance to discern what he did when things work better. This is the perfectionist who stifles his free voice by constantly trying to fix things like an artist who cannot finish a painting.

- The Authentic Singer knows she is 100 percent responsible for everything that happens. Good or bad she takes ownership and learns accordingly. If her performance was not stellar because she was battling bad acoustics, she learns to let go of expectations and not push her voice next time. If the conductor takes a piece too slowly, she learns not to panic and plans for contingency breaths in future performances. She enjoys her successes and graciously accepts compliments but learns not to expect success every time. She knows all she can do is simply prepare thoroughly and always do her best.

The Diva's way of blaming external factors is very common and understandable. We feel that if we admit our failures we are weakening ourselves and will suffer because of it. But we weaken only the image of ourselves, our ego, and the person we think we *should* be, not our true, authentic self. We have all heard the saying We only learn from our failures. But we can only learn from failures if we open ourselves to admitting them. Only by this learning can we actually strengthen our core and open up more possibilities for dealing with problems in the future.

The Introvert's constant self-blame and perfectionism blinds him from growth through success. Contrary to popular belief, I think we also learn from our successes, if we pay careful attention to how they came about. But we must be prepared to watch carefully the big picture of what is happening when things go right, not constantly be distracted by the tiny flaws. Otherwise we miss the main road of our journey, sent on a detour of analysis, destructive self-criticism, and false expectations.

We must learn to recognize our successes and our failures and acknowledge them as such, without judging ourselves by them. It is clear, then, that giving the Authentic Singer already inside you its voice is the most powerful step you can take toward becoming the singer you want to be.

"Out beyond ideas of right- and wrongdoing there is a field—
I'll meet you there." – Rumi

PRACTICE:

- *Become aware of the Judge.* You need to look him in the eye if you are to command him out of your life! Listen to what he says and when he says it. If you catch yourself cursing when you run out of breath at the end of a phrase, take a deep breath and be calm. Ask yourself what you must do next time to fix the problem. Do you need an extra breath somewhere or is there a way to extend your air? If a note cracks or wobbles or is off pitch, do you know what to do to fix it or should you ask your teacher for help? Instead of getting angry or frustrated or upset, just ask questions of your Adviser. That way, you are more likely to find a solution. Questions, not judgments, lead you forward on your path.

- *Listen to lots of different singers.* Listen to ones you know you like, ones you have not liked in the past, and ones you don't know. Listen *with discernment.* Listen *in detail.* Without judging, determine what you like and what you don't like about each voice. What are the elements that bring you to the conclusions you have? Write down your thoughts. Can you hear vulnerabilities in the voices you like? Can you discern qualities you had missed in the voices you didn't like? When you concentrate on the things you do like, do the qualities you weren't so drawn to fade into the background somewhat? Can you, in other words, manipulate what you *hear* by what you *think?* (An interesting exercise for us all, and further evidence of the power of the mind.) Use your experience of listening to other singers to help you to hear your own voice differently and maybe to hear more of the positive rather than the negative aspects. (More on this in chapter 8.) You probably will discern as you listen to more and more singers that in the imperfection of most singing lies the humanity which is, in fact, its great strength.

- *Make notes in your voice lessons (or afterward) about what sign-posts your teacher has put up for you.* In what direction is he pointing? What does he seem to discern are the problems you have at the moment? Are you listening to what you need to do to improve? Or are you only listening for signs of approval to feed your ego? Don't be afraid to feed back to your teacher what you are hearing him say and check with him to see if you are correct in your understanding. In other words, that you are *hearing* what he is trying to tell you. In this way you can determine whether your Judge or your perception of your teacher's Judge is getting in the way of communication between you.

- *Visualize your path toward your goal as horizontal not vertical.* Stop thinking in terms of reaching the top, climbing, or striving and substitute moving forward, growing, or taking steps toward.

- *Try to listen for the truth behind the comments and suggestions listeners may give.* When someone gives you feedback on a performance, there may well be a superficial layer of judgment coming from their own egos but be aware that underneath that you may well be able to discern an authentic voice offering valuable advice. Look for the seed of truth from which to grow.

- *Learn to take compliments graciously* (perhaps with a smile and a simple "Thank you very much"). Don't dismiss positive feedback or respond negatively. ("Oh, I thought it was terrible today. I can do much better.") That's your Judge talking, and your aim is to silence him! When you dismiss compliments like this, you push them out of consciousness as well as shutting down the compliment giver, who may have more of value to say. We can often learn something from positive feedback, if our discerning antennae are raised.

- *Be aware also that your listeners may not be judging you at all.* They may be totally forgiving and undemanding. But don't use that as an excuse to relinquish your responsibility *to yourself* to do your very best. You will never be satisfied if you "cheat" your audience. Being less than committed or honest with any listeners will compromise your own happiness and satisfaction. Be respectful of your audience. Everyone deserves your best performance.

- *Treat practicing singing like a scientific experiment.* Try things out and play around with your voice. If it is just an experiment, then when things work you can simply repeat it the next time you need it—as long as you were paying attention when you did it. But if things go wrong with your experiment, you are simply able to say to yourself "That didn't work" and try something else, just as a scientist in his laboratory would. You remain objective and honest about your voice, unemotional and detached from the outcome. You are simply observing. When your experiment leads you to a big breakthrough, by all means allow yourself the opportunity to rejoice. This is, after all, the gift of happiness singing can give!

- *Stay present in every moment of your singing.* As I will say many times, this is the surest way to eliminate self-judgment and develop discernment.

Finally, the very best way to improve at anything is not to judge yourself to be bad in the first place. Simply seek to be better. Then, as you improve, you will be inspired to be even better.

Firm, hard goals that we try to fast-forward to reach are terrible distractions from our small steps forward, and are likely to lead us into accidents; we may miss the steps we need to take to reach the goal, because we are so focused on getting there. We will be constantly judging ourselves against that goal, and it is inevitable that we will not be able live up to the comparison. "Not good enough! Not good enough!" will scream the voice. So instead of focusing on your goal, simply take a glimpse at where you want to go and then put your destination to the back of your mind as you begin to focus on the slow steps toward it. Check the steps as you take them. Was that better? Am I moving in the right direction? Do I need to do something different? Should I take another path? Don't allow the Judge to emerge. Remind yourself that *all* experience is valuable once you decide that the *experience* is your path and your way forward. *Good* or *bad* have no relevance any more, as you focus on "Where do I go from here?" or "Where would I like to be next?" Then, perhaps, you'll find yourself at your goal in no time, only to discover that it is just another step on your journey.

Eliminate the Judge from your singing life.

Chapter 6

On Air

Trusting the Breath

"The breath is the meeting place of the mind and the body."
– Patsy Rodenburg, *The Right to Speak*

Aspire: *to reach for, desire eagerly; from the Latin* aspirare, *meaning to breathe toward.*

Inspire*: to influence an experience of increased energy and creativity; from the Latin* inspirare, meaning *to breathe in.*

Spirit: *vital principle; the soul; enthusiasm, activating emotion; from the Latin,* spiritus, *meaning breath.*

Looking at the words above, we notice the direct connection breath has to so many aspects of our creative life. In the West, we tend to pay little attention to it in the normal course of things. We breathe naturally and habitually. But it is worth noting that breathing is one of the few physical functions that is both involuntary and under our voluntary control. The voluntary aspect is very important for a singer to understand.

When we think of vocal technique often the first thing that springs to mind is breathing. Most students come to me having either no idea about breathing for singing or with a crisis because of it. However, breath is not just part of the vocal mechanism, something we must control to produce a good sound or to get through a long phrase; it is also the connection between ourselves and the song.

My intention here is to return your attention to the breath. It may seem we can abandon the breath once it feels as though it is working comfortably, so our focus can shift to other things like creating expressive tone or communicating effectively. However we soon realize that the breath is the influential element at the heart of all these things. It is, essentially, the *heart of singing*. Not only is it "the meeting place of the mind and the body," as Patsy Rodenburg suggests, but it also carries with it our emotional relationship to the song we are singing. If we forget to come back to the breath with awareness, the link between body, mind, and emotions that our breath forms can easily weaken and even break.

As I discussed in chapter 1, it is partly the close association of singing to breath that gives our voice its power over the listener. To take full control of that power, the singer must understand the breath in all its aspects. In this chapter, I intend to help you look at breath and breathing not by teaching you some new technique but simply by viewing it from different angles and giving you a new perspective on why what you *do* learn about breath in your voice lessons is so vital.

What We Are Taught

There is some controversy around the approach to breath in voice teaching. There is one school of thought that steers singers completely away from focusing too much attention on breathing. I remember one of my teachers telling me not to even think about the breath because being obsessed with breath control caused more harm than good. He believed that when everything else was right, the breath would take care of itself.

In his book *Singing and Imagination,* Thomas Hemsley quotes Sims Reeves "Incorrect breathing is an acquired habit, induced sometimes by an elaborate means taken to avoid it. A few simple hints are all that is necessary: the rest of what is called the art of breathing is very much a matter of instinct." Hemsley goes on to add "Bad breathing habits are usually either acquired (often from the instructions of some 'breath faddist' teacher), the direct result of bad posture, or the result of the singer's inability to imagine the music in large." In other words, the breath works perfectly well if you do not interfere with it or when it is well instructed by thought. There is definitely truth to this theory. Certainly much harm can be done by overworking the breath or by a student's obsession with the length of phrase she can sing. Breath and its management in singing is only the means to an end and not the end itself; focusing solely on this aspect of technique can become obsessive and lead us way off our path.

A second school of thought on this matter takes the opposite approach. The "breath faddists," as Hemsley calls them, believe control of the breath must be drilled into the student and many hours of exercise are necessary to teach the body what it must do because breathing for singing is different from our normal breathing habits. They may spend weeks working on breath control, strengthening the breathing muscles, and doing breath management exercises before allowing the student to even sing a note. The image of a singer lying with piles of heavy books on his stomach or Caruso's famed ability to move a grand piano with his diaphragm and abdominal muscles comes to mind. I can sympathize with this school of thought, too; it would indeed be dangerous for any singer to underestimate the power and importance of the breath. We must have the strength and control of the muscles involved to make the breath and the voice work efficiently. We must understand what the breath does, how to use it successfully, and experience its power to get to the point where we trust it— something that is essential for any singer.

What do we make of this conflict of ideas? I've acknowledged the positive aspects of both sides, but both schools of thought also have their drawbacks. With the first you run the risk of never thoroughly understanding the breath and then struggling with control all the time. With the second you are in danger of restricting the breath's freedom by being too obsessed with its control and losing track of other vital components that make up great singing. So I suggest that what we need to do is find how to bring both ways to a balanced middle ground without losing the good aspects from each. We pay attention to working on breathing technique and understanding the importance of the breath but don't lose sight of our goal—to be able to forget about it and let it be free to do its work.

BREATH IN TECHNIQUE

It is my conviction that a majority of all the technical problems we have in singing, including most performance disasters, stem from improper use of the breath or a breakdown in its control. Either we misuse it or forget to use it where we need it or try to control it from the wrong place or don't fully trust it or push it beyond its limits or end up out of control because there isn't enough breath left to do its job in the singing process. All singers will have experienced that feeling of the tightening of the throat, the panic that sets in, and the feeling of helplessness as a pitch falters or tone deteriorates because air is running out. I do not intend to go into detail about breath management here or give numerous examples of breathing exercises[7]. That I leave to your voice teacher. But I would like to share some general theories I have about the breath in technique to give you a few things to consider:

First, here are some definitions of *control*:

- *The power to influence behavior or the course of events* (author's emphasis)
- The restriction of an activity or phenomenon
- A means of limiting or *regulating something* (author's emphasis)

As I've emphasized above, when we sing we must have the power to influence the course of the airflow and find the optimum way to regulate it. Restriction of the breath is a dangerous thing and limiting the breath essentially leads to limiting our vocal potential. The *control* we need over the breath has to do primarily with the exhalation—the quality (pace, pressure, etc.) of the flow of air we let out. The inhalation should in effect not be *controlled* but *allowed* to happen. We open ourselves—our bodies—to the inflow of air but take control of the outflow. The key is *opening ourselves fully* to the inhaled breath.

Opening the Body to the Breath: The Deep Inhalation

As most singers are aware, singing well demands the use of the diaphragmatic breath: as air enters the body the diaphragm

---

7   Some of the best breathing exercises I have come across in print are not in a singing manual but in Patsy Rodenburg's excellent book *The Right to Speak*, which is about the use of the speaking voice.

lowers, the abdomen expands outward, and the ribcage widens and rises slightly. We also experience a slight expansion around the back. There are very good physical reasons why we need to find a way to this deep inhalation.

Firstly, diaphragmatic breathing is physiologically the most efficient way we can breathe. It takes breath to the lower part of the lungs where there are more alveoli (air cells) and therefore more opportunity for oxygen transfer to the blood. The more oxygen in the blood, the less frequently we feel the need to breathe. So having taken a deeper breath, not only do we have more air at our disposal for our singing, but we also retard the body's demand for more oxygen. Secondly, in using the muscles of the diaphragm and abdomen to expel the air, rather than the intercostals and the collapsing of the rib cage, we have much better control over the outflow.

It is, however, quite usual for students to come to me breathing by means of what is known as the *paradoxical* breath. Instead of the abdominal muscles relaxing and moving outward as the breath flows in, they tense and squeeze in, pushing against the descending diaphragm. The chest expands, allowing some air into the lungs, but the inflowing breath quickly hits a barrier when it meets the inhibited diaphragm. This obviously is not an efficient breathing technique, so what is happening here?

There could be a simple explanation rooted in our physical habits. This may be just the same habitual breath most people use all day for speaking but magnified. When a voice teacher asks the student to breathe deeply, he simply exaggerates what he always does when he inhales. (Sadly our breathing instincts since we got out of the cradle and stood on two feet have not been necessarily the healthiest or best, though perhaps the easiest.) If you have had any voice lessons, you will have learned that this type of paradoxical breathing will not work for efficient singing, so it's vital that you cure yourself of this bad habit quickly.

BREATH AND OUR SELF-IMAGE

There may be another reason preventing us from breathing into the deep place. It has to do with body image.

We are bombarded today with images of "perfect" bodies—men with broad, muscular shoulders, narrow hips and waist, and six-pack abs, and women with slender bodies and flat stomachs. Many of us consciously or unconsciously aspire to emulate those images. But when we breathe to sing, we suddenly have to take that deep breath that expands our stomachs, creating the disturbing feeling for many of being "fat". I have had numerous students who initially simply cannot let go of the tension in their stomachs because they habitually hold them in. It may take months for them to feel comfortable with the deep, singing breath. One young woman, a dancer, had been so obsessed with flattening her stomach that she would do 250 crunches and sit-ups in one daily session. Not only did she completely inhibit her breathing, but in the end had to have surgery to correct intestinal problems she had created! When she recovered and stopped her excessive regime, she discovered with glee how much easier her singing was when she was able to open up to her deep breath.

Great singing requires that we let go of our egos, and that includes in the realm of body image. And as with so many aspects of our art, when you release yourself from the shackles of how you believe you *should* be, stop pandering to the expectations of others, and simply follow the way to be the best singer you can be, suddenly you gain the happiness and satisfaction you were looking for in the first place. Allowing your deep breath is the first step.

THE QUALITY OF THE EXHALATION

There is a way of breathing
That's a shame and a suffocation
And there's another way of expiring,
A love breath,
That lets you open infinitely

– Rumi

In the act of singing, our breath is all powerful on its way out of our bodies. What it does, how it flows, and where it goes will influence the sound we produce. We must remember that the vocal mechanism is very delicate and can easily be set off balance. Initially this powerful breath must be gently applied, so that things are set up carefully rather than shock the system. Even if we want to sing loudly or powerfully, we must almost always initiate the sound gently.

I liken this to a Japanese calligrapher with his brush; he dips his fat brush into the ink that causes the bristles to come together in the finest point. After making a decision about how wide he needs his stroke to be, he applies the tip of his brush to the paper or canvas, with a very gentle touch. If he wants his line to be wide and bold, he leans into the brush and a broad stroke appears. With an even, carefully controlled flow, he creates his character, and when that is done, he gently lifts his brush away from the canvas. If at any point the calligrapher jerks, pushes too hard, or hesitates, the result is an uneven flow of ink that will spoil the image. The breath could be seen to be working in the same way as the brush. We must approach every phrase with a narrow thread of breath (even if we are preparing to sing loudly), set up the vital balance and resonance, and then "lean into" the breath to create the required dynamic, carefully regulating the flow as we carry on through the vocal line, gently lifting off the thread of breath once more as we end. With practice, this "threading" takes so little time that the listener is not even aware of it, except to feel the comfortable balance achieved. If we jerk or push too hard too soon or hesitate with our breath, our vocal "canvas" is ruined with splatters.

TRUSTING THE BREATH

It is worth remembering that *singing is a beautiful and powerful manifestation of the breath transformed.* I believe the "beauty and power" of our singing is rooted in the trust we place in the breath.

Once we have the beginning of the breath, we then make our decision about the *rate* of flow (for instance, the stronger the flow, the louder the sound) and the *quality* of flow (an even flow for legato singing and short puffs for detached notes, etc.) *Where* the breath goes once it is on its path is controlled to some extent by our thought (thought of placement, for example) and our technique (opening or closing paths to resonance). However, the control we take even here must be to a certain degree limited; we also have to trust the breath itself. To work most efficiently, the breath needs freedom to seek out the best places, the most vibrations, and does not take kindly to interference in this. Not trusting that the breath will do this, many singers feel they must keep on giving it a "helping hand" by tightening muscles along the way, effectively shutting down resonance pathways. We have therefore first to control the breath from the right place but then learn to *minimize* that control once the breath is on its way. Like the kite flier, we keep hold of the string, but let the kite dance.

The problem we encounter is that the Controller tells the voice/breath how it *should* be. Maybe you have heard a voice you wish you had. Or maybe there is a voice inside your head that is the one you think you have but doesn't seem to want to come out. The Controller will be quick to tell you that how your voice sounds now is not right and needs to be different. The ego loves to leap to judge, but it is not good at all at offering a solution. Only your Adviser offers solutions, but, as we've discussed, its advice typically goes unheeded.

The Adviser would say that the secret to breath efficiency is to *allow* the breath to do its job and *allow* the voice to be itself—*your* voice from *your* body. Let it be.

I see it like riding a horse. We sit on the beautiful beast's back and indicate through means of our body language and muscle use what we would like the horse to do. We take control. If we want to go faster, we set the horse off on a gallop by physical (and perhaps vocal) signals, and we avoid falling off by technique. But we must free the horse to find its own rhythm and use its own power. We take control of what we truly can control and must trust our horse for the rest. Just as the horse knows how to gallop, the singing breath knows how to find resonance spaces and create vibration.

The idea then is to initiate the breath flow from deep down and take *subtle* control with gentle persuasion from the diaphragm and abdominal muscles. Be sure to stay aware of the breath (as we do the horse) in case we feel its need for minor correction to keep it on its path, but in the meantime, dare to allow the breath "free rein."

THE EMOTIONAL CONNECTION

The use of the diaphragmatic breath in singing is not only necessary for the sake of having enough breath to sing a phrase or taking control of the pitch. That same breath is needed to tap into and express our core emotions.

In his book *Using Voice and Movement in Therapy,* Paul Newham of the London Voice Centre explains that during the act of deep inhalation a connection is set up with physical and emotional sensations located all the way down to the lower abdomen. In the process of deep breathing, we physically set up a "psychological process with deep emotional implications."

Think for a moment about our deepest, instinctual feelings. We grab at our bellies whenever we experience extreme states of emotion; when we laugh hysterically, sob in grief, or moan in ecstasy our voices come from a place very deep down in our gut. Often these are not easy emotions for us to experience or at least share with the world, perhaps because we are afraid of the loss of control they threaten. So we teach ourselves to control them. It has been shown through monitored experiments that many people immobilize the diaphragm to contain expressions of aggression or other powerful feelings to keep them out of consciousness. We may also inhibit our vocal tract[8] to close down the pathway for the air. The deep place we need our breath to go to take control of its outflow for singing is a very scary place for most people.

It is not surprising then that when we do breathe correctly to sing, we find ourselves tapping into surprisingly strong emotions. In class after class that I have led, in workshops where I've used deep breathing, focusing exercises, and encouraged my students to truly open up to that deep place, I have been amazed how easily students find themselves weeping. Of course we are going

---

8   *Vocal tract* refers to the tubal space between our lips and our larynx and the internal moveable parts (including the tongue and soft palate) that can be manipulated to alter resonance.

to avoid going there. It is so much easier to stay in our heads, in our intellect, in our left brains, and work it all out from there. That way we stay in control. But if we can't allow the free inflow of breath, the very first physical thing we must do to sing at all, we are never going to completely free our voice as it goes out into the world. We will never truly allow ourselves to uncover the singer we want to be.

I mentioned in chapter 2 that some voice teachers were opposed to taking students too far into emotional realms since it opens up psychological and emotional paths down which they may not be qualified to lead. But if you truly want to succeed, you are going to have to be prepared for some struggle, some hard work, and even, possibly, some emotional revelations because *that is where singing takes us.* This part of your singing path may be left for you to tread alone.

WORKING WITH THE EMOTIONAL BREATH

The connection between breath flow and emotions is something the singer must become acutely aware of. Without acknowledging and understanding this connection, the singer may never fully express his experience of his songs.

The breath conveys and frees our emotions by its nature, and its quality changes as our emotions change. We can also switch things around and change our breath pattern to change our emotional response. Imagine a moment of great agitation or excitement, and you'll find the breath is shallow and fast. Break the pattern by taking deeper breaths and slowing the breathing down, and you begin to calm down. This is part of the power we must tap into as singers. If we don't understand or acknowledge the role of breath in emotional response, we will encounter problems communicating our message and miss great opportunities for connecting with our audience, as well as with ourselves.

Actors learn that the nature of their own response to the situation they are playing inevitably changes the quality and flow of their breath, or, as I said, the nature of the breath changes the emotion. What is actually happening is that the breath is simply responding to thought, which is the emotional trigger. It affects the inhalation as well as the exhalation. The inhalation contains the full emotion of the words that follow it. In other words, the quality of the inhalation alters according to its emotional trigger. The exhalation then carries that response as an expression to the listener. For a singer this can be a very difficult concept, since the breath in singing has been taught as a tool for creation of a particular sound not a particular emotion. In performing a song, the singer first has to learn breath management simply to keep pitch and support the musical line. For many singers this is a huge task in itself and, once accomplished, may seem like the end of their work.

But now we must learn to convey emotions by the nature of the outflow of air. We are asking the breath for two seemingly opposing things here: to create a beautiful (or at least supported) singing tone and good pitch, and to express emotions that are usually conveyed on a breath that is *incapable of doing that*. This is not an impossible situation, however. When we begin to allow our breath the freedom to express the emotions that naturally flow through it and reach down into our core to give vent to those emotions, we may be surprised how all aspects of the voice come together. Technique does not have to be compromised by using the breath honestly.

An accomplished singer can convey changes of emotion through the breath and still present a supported, beautiful voice. Listen to any great opera or jazz singer, and you hear the breath at work, constantly in flow, and constantly changing how the voice sounds. These great artists do it by being flexible in the way they use their breath, and staying creative in imagining what sounds they can or need to convey to communicate fully. They may use the breath with a different approach at the beginning of a note or phrase to momentarily present an emotion, only pulling in full support and tone once the feeling has been established for the listener. The art of using the breath can be subtle and complex. Be aware that only by returning to the breath and working with it regularly will you find ways to develop its full potential.

Deep Breathing and Health

It may encourage you to know that the deep singing breath is in fact very good for you. There are marked health benefits associated with diaphragmatic breathing. It has been used along with relaxation exercises in treating anxiety and has been shown to help lower blood pressure and strengthen the immune system when practiced on a daily basis. Because of its close connection to our emotions, deep breathing can be used successfully for such things as anger management or control of addictions. Yoga breathing exercises (*pranayama*) have been used for centuries to calm *or* energize the body and focus the mind. As we have seen, the deep breath is central to meditation. I have often wondered if one of the reasons so many people have a desire to sing is linked to their unconscious understanding of the healthful aspects of breathing deeply and allowing vibrations into their bodies. Could it be that our Adviser is telling us it's good for us to sing?

Practicing with the Breath:

Here are a few things you can do to help strengthen your trust in and control of the breath.

- *Notice your breathing throughout the day.* Monitor how it changes with your mood and emotions. Become aware of it. Be prepared to allow your breath to be as expressive in song as it is in your daily life.

- *Begin to be aware of subtle restrictions in your body as you inhale.* Look for the barriers you may have erected to prevent the deep breath. Practice releasing the unnecessary tensions and allow yourself to relax as you breathe in. Go back to your meditation exercises to put you in touch with your breath.

- *Practice using the breath in different ways.* Stay flexible about your breathing technique. Bad habits creep into breathing easier than any other aspect of singing, so don't cling to one way of doing it *if it's not working.* Look for breathing exercises in various publications not just in books on singing[9]. These exercises may not always be the exact *technique* to use while singing, but they will expand your experience of the breathing mechanism and enhance flexibility.

- *Acknowledge its power. Breath is the essential, living center of singing and is at its very heart.* I don't think many would disagree with that. It is the connector between our technique and our emotions; it births our tone, volume, and expressiveness. In doing so, it also frees our creativity. Nothing happens without it working efficiently. When we recognize this power, we understand that we cannot turn our attention away from the breath until we know *that it will be our instinct to use it correctly.*

- *Envision the brush of the calligrapher and approach beginning and ending notes so as not to "splat."* Become aware of the breath at the moment the sound starts and ends. Sing one note at a time and observe.

- *Understand the power of your imagination/mind.* Be aware that the breath is as much controlled by the mind as the body. Once your physical control of the breath is encoded in your body, you can enhance that control even more with your thoughts. "Thinking to the end of the phrase" is a typical call of many coaches for musical and expressive reasons but having the whole phrase you are about to sing in your mind before you sing it also has a profound effect on the amount of air you will use as you go. Your mind, as well as your body, is then working to monitor how much air you use at any given moment, bearing in mind what is still to come. There will also be times when the power of your mind manifests in ways that may not be so helpful. You may have practiced a particular phrase so many times and *not* achieved what you wanted with the breath that

---

9   Patsy Rodenburg's *The Right to Speak,* which I mentioned earlier, or a good book on yoga breathing would be places to start.

focusing on *trying* to make it only brings up bad memories of previous attempts that failed. You didn't make it work then, so your mind doesn't believe you will succeed this time. At times like that, you can experiment with the "distraction method" of breath management. Instead of concentrating on the breath, you distract it with thoughts of something else like the emotional drive of the song or articulating the words clearly. I must emphasize that you should resort to this only when you are otherwise breathing instinctively correctly and efficiently. It is a technique for the time when it is a habit of the mind that is inhibiting your success. The habit must be broken and such a distraction often works to show you that you can do it after all, if you just let go of the *trying*.

- *In practice, try to sing songs or exercises of different tempi and moods to allow the breath to work at different paces.* I always feel the best way to have the breath work well is to inhale in the tempo of the song you're about to sing. For a faster tempo, your inhalation will be quicker or shorter (not shallower); for a slower song, you will give more time for the inhalation to fall into the body. When you do this, you will notice the quick inhalation has an energizing effect, maybe quickening the pulse, and the slow inhalation has a calming effect. Your whole body is then aligned to the mood and pace of the song.

- *Experiment with fully connecting to your emotions.* Tap into how your breath changes according to those emotions and try singing on that transformed breath flow. It may be difficult at first to find a good tone or supported pitch when you are feeling great sadness to the point of weeping or enormous anger that tends to shut the throat, but with practice, you can find a way to keep the necessary energy for singing at the center of your breath flow, while the emotional dimensions are, in effect, layered on top. It may take some practice, but for the singer who wants to be a solo performer and truly reach the heart of the song and convey it to his audience, it is essential to do this.

(I will go into more detail about dealing with emotions in singing in chapter 9.) Make sure the breath flow reflects and conveys your feelings.

- *Look for places in a song where you could use your breath to great effect by applying it differently.* Sigh into the note or vary the length of phrases or intensify the breath or even make your sound breathy. Listen to the way good singers use their breath as a means of expression. Notice that on occasion "breath in the sound" can take precedence over full resonance as the desirable quality for the sake of conveying emotion or style. Play with your breath, as an artist plays with different ways to touch his brush to the canvas. Stay flexible and nonjudgmental about the range of sounds you allow yourself to make; not every one of them has to be beautiful to be expressive. Value all sounds as being potential expressions of your Authentic Voice. Then choose from your color palette!

Remember that your breath is inherent in *inspiring* your creativity, giving courage to your singing *spirit,* and being the catalyst that leads you to become the singer you *aspire* to be!

It's all about breathing.
Trust the breath.

CHAPTER 7

LET'S GET PHYSICAL

ATTENDING TO THE BODY

"A healthy body is a guest-chamber for the soul;
a sick body is a prison."
— Francis Bacon

SINGING AS A WHOLE-BODY ACTIVITY

To find a way to the full expression of yourself and to fully experience the benefits of singing, you must be prepared to use your whole body in the process. As I have emphasized over and over in this book, full commitment is the path to freeing your voice and freeing yourself. Our body is our instrument. We must learn to use it as a whole, not only play on one string.

When you sing, your entire body becomes a sounding board for the vibrating vocal folds, much like the body of the cello enhances the meager sound of vibrating strings. You are the vessel that must resonate to create your unique voice. With this in mind, before you begin to sing, you have to take a good look at your own physical habits. It is vital to find good alignment of the spine, loosen the shoulders, release tension in the neck and jaw, and so on, so that your instrument (your whole body) is aligned and ready for the task.

The details of correct posture and physical actions I shall leave up to your teacher, who can observe you and make recommendations. There are also many singing manuals and books that will help you with understanding the physical aspects of singing. My task here is to make you more aware of the whole, remind you of your role in addressing your own physical problems, and touch on a few aspects that sometimes get overlooked.

BECOMING PHYSICALLY AWARE

If you look carefully around any group of people you will notice a variety of physical habits created by years of conditioning: shoulders pushed forward or too far back, spine slumped, chin pulled in, hips pushed forward, slouching sideways onto one hip, and many other misalignments and tensions that are adopted for any variety of reasons. A young woman holding her shoulders forward with her arms across her body may have formed the habit in the process of physical development. As her breasts grew, she needed to disguise her transformation into a woman, deny her sexuality (consciously or unconsciously), and so altered her body posture to hide herself as much as possible. On the other hand, a man with shoulders locked back may have taken on the posture to portray strength and dominance, attempting to enhance his stature by "puffing out his chest." Someone with a slumped spine could simply have a lazy posture or may be doing their best to appear small and insignificant, or, if he is particularly tall, he may be trying to lower himself to an average person's eye level. The reasons may be psychological, social, or personal, but we all have similar habits, and they are habits that have a direct influence on the voice in speech and singing.

BEING PRESENT: BODY CONSCIOUSNESS

Just as we must address vocal problems openly and honestly and without judgment, so we must also learn to look at our physical selves in the same way.

Give yourself a chance to get to know your physical self more intimately.

- Observe yourself in a full-length mirror, or, if possible, two mirrors, so you can see yourself from all angles. Look honestly and openly and without judgment. (It's best to do this either in underwear (or not!) or in form-fitting clothes to make it easier to see the details. Remember, no judgment!) Stand up tall, as if you are about to sing. Simply observe any physical bad habits that seem to put you out of alignment. You may notice a slight sideward curve in your spine or a dropped shoulder. You may see your head cocked slightly to one side. If you turn sideways you may notice your lower back collapsed making your behind and stomach stick out. Make adjustments if you can and observe how it feels. Close your eyes for a few seconds and focus on the place you made the adjustment. Breathe deeply a few times concentrating on the spot. Open your eyes and check once again that the correction is made. Walk around a bit and come back to the mirror in the adjusted position. (This may be even easier if you have a friend to observe you and give you honest feedback about these things. Remind them you won't take it personally!)

- Stay in front of the mirror and sing something easy. Don't worry about the sound, just be aware of what happens physically. What do you see? Do you push your jaw to one side or jut it forward as you sing? Do you put your head down or pull it back? What is happening to your body when you inhale? Are your hands and knees loose? Be very detailed in your examination and write down some observations. If you are unclear about the correctness of some of your habits, take the list to your teacher and ask about them. If you see something you know needs correcting, try making the change and observe what happens when you consciously don't allow it to happen. How do you sound? How do you feel?

- Ask someone you can trust to be honest to tell you about your physical habits when he sees you perform. Are there movements that could distract an audience and are disconnected from the song you are singing? Open yourself to accepting observations of your physical habits and remember not to take them as judgments. Understand that it can be very difficult for some people to give you the feedback you seek, so reassure everyone who hears or watches you that you are looking for honesty.

Some of our habits are easy to let go of. Some prove very difficult to release. As with everything, awareness is the first step to addressing our physical habits.

Body Focus

I use the term *body focus* to describe the state the body needs to be in for us to be able to sing our best. I've described how important mind focus is in the singing process, but however concentrated your mind, your instrument is not going to soar unless the body is also focused on its task. I have had students who are mentally very alert and present, keenly observing their voices, noticing what their breath is doing, or what they are feeling in a particular song, but who are oblivious to what is happening in their bodies. Without even knowing it, they may sway from side to side or fidget with their hands or lean backward as they approach a high note or shift their balance to one foot or jerk their head backward as they inhale. I had one student who shook her head like a horse whinnying every time she took a breath. Her singing sometimes sounded just like the horse, too! I pointed it out to her, and, as is usually the case, she was completely unaware of it. It took several months of constant reminder to release the habit, but with patience, she did it, and her voice began to strengthen, and her support stabilized.

It is important to rid ourselves of any superfluous actions and physical habits that do not enhance and may even detract from our singing. Our bodies should be performing only the essential tasks our singing requires, particularly as we are learning what *is* essential. At this stage we are programming our "singing computer," that is body and brain, to be as efficient as possible, and we need to peel off the layers of distractions from our central task.

I don't mean to suggest that we can never do anything outside the singing process when we sing. Of course, if we are on stage in any capacity, in opera, musical theater or any performance, we rarely stand completely still and do nothing. Even a choir member may be asked to move in some way to enhance a performance. But whatever we do must not be in the "computer program" as something associated with the actual technique of singing. When we move as we sing, whatever we do must be an essential part of the *performance*, but must not in any way disturb the core of our singing. When we have that core strengthened by discovering exactly what we *do* need to do to sing our best, our bodies are free to express the song in any way at all because that core will still be at our command.

So as you inhale in readiness to sing, make sure that your body, as well as your mind, comes into focus. This moment of preparation is enormously important for the singer and must not be overlooked. Think of it like the orchestral conductor's upbeat: without it, the orchestra would be incapable of playing the first chords together as no one would know the tempo or when to begin. The result would be a musical mess. Your singing body is like an orchestra, made up of many parts that must all come together to be capable of singing efficiently and beautifully. If you fail to focus your mind and body on the task you are about to perform, you will no doubt end up with a singing mess! So as you take your first breath, think of it as pulling together all the separate strands of physical energy in your body and gathering them together into a strong, central column through which your expressive voice flows.

This core strength must remain in focus as you continue singing, though this can be an elusive state, as we can be so easily distracted by the sound of our own voice (or the voice of the Judge). So let's look at how to prepare your body to focus and hopefully develop physical habits that aid, rather than hinder, your path to successful singing.

FROM THE GROUND UP...

The ground itself (and our relationship to it) is very significant in the art of singing. As singers, we spend so much time thinking about sound, and things happening from the neck upward that this important relationship is often forgotten or ignored. We don't sing with our feet, so why pay the ground any attention at all? Well, without its roots anchored, the tree cannot stand, and the leaves cannot grow. Without its grounding, the voice cannot soar. Lack of grounding not only manifests itself in the sound of the voice but also in how the singer looks to an observer. Is she unsteady in her posture, maybe swaying or constantly shifting balance? Does she move away from her own center? An ungrounded singer often gives the impression that she wants to run away, that she doesn't want to be singing right now, and that she has nothing of importance or relevance to say. This is not the image that will keep an audience riveted!

So we must learn to love that natural force that stops us from flying away. Gravity is our friend. We don't allow it to drag us down or cause us to collapse in a heap, but we can use it greatly to our benefit as an antagonistic force against which we balance our upward and outward vocal energy that sends our voices into the world.

Try this exercise to find your ground:

- Stand with your feet about shoulder distance apart. Keep your head level and your eyes looking forward. Be sure your shoulders and arms are relaxed. Imagine that there is a strong force pushing up from the ground through your feet, trying to launch you into the air. Bend your knees slightly and visualize an energy flowing from your rear, down your legs, and through the balls of your feet that is pushing down against that force. At the same time, feel as though you pull your spine up out of your hips, elongating it all the way up through your neck, without allowing your head to tilt. Just imagine these energies in opposition to each other. What happens if you let go of the downward push against the imagined upward thrust? You probably feel a rush of upward energy, losing your feeling of being grounded and having a sense of flying out of control. That is exactly what will happen to your voice if you fail to stay grounded. Go back to focusing on resisting the imagined force and regain your ground. Repeat the exercise with your eyes closed and become aware of how it feels to be perfectly grounded.

Once you are fully grounded, you may well discover that it is not only the audience that then perceives you as a singer with something important to convey; you will begin to believe it yourself.

THE BALANCING ACT

Along with grounding, we need a perfect sense of balance. Balance is such an important concept in singing that I have devoted a whole chapter to it later in the book, but it is important here that we address physical balance. Singing while the body is struggling to stay upright is never going to be efficient and will lead to numerous vocal problems.

- Take a grounded stance as above. Keeping your feet in place, slowly sway your whole body as far as possible to the left until you are about to fall—but don't! Then swing back through the center and all the way to the right. When you reach the farthest point right, come back to the center. Feel the comfort and safety of arriving back in that middle place. Do the same sort of exercise leaning first far forward on your toes, then way back through your heels, and then back to the middle, grounding yourself once more through the front center of your feet. This gives you the sense of where your central fulcrum is and brings you to your balance "home."

We may learn the ideal way to stand for singing, but that ideal may not always be available to us. For instance, if we are on stage in opera or musical theater we may have to sing in all sorts of physical positions, few of which look anything like ideal[10]. But if you can learn grounding and balance, you can take the central home with you whatever you are doing around it. Our task here is to not let that core strength get knocked off track, and that takes a certain amount of practice. The following exercise helps to expand our balance awareness and strengthen our sense of grounding, giving us more security in our singing.

- Take your grounded, balanced stance. Close your eyes and breathe deep into your belly. Now imagine that with

10   The old days of "stand-and-sing" opera are long gone, and directors have been known to ask singers to perform difficult arias lying down, leaning over, or even upside down. I was once in an opera production where the soprano was required to sing an immensely demanding aria full of high Cs while swinging from a rope!

every breath each leg is filling with sand; continue until each leg is half full and weighted down. You should feel perfectly balanced and grounded. Open your eyes and fix on a point straight ahead. Now you are going to shift the weight very slowly to your left foot. Your knee must be slightly bent at this point. Imagine releasing all the sand from your right leg and letting it pour into the left. Now your right leg is completely weightless, and your whole balance is shifted to your left leg and down through your foot. Stand on one foot for a few seconds or longer, focusing your mind and energy down through the center of your foot. Inhale slowly and deeply. If you wobble and lose your balance, just take the stance again, ground yourself once more, and adjust your posture until you can remain almost still with all your weight on one foot for three deep breaths. Now take a very slow step forward imagining once again the steady transfer of sand (weight) from one leg to the other, making sure you allow the transfer to be complete before you lift your other foot off the ground. Walk a few steps in this very slow fashion. Focus on the action of walking. When you are fully focused and in flow, try singing something simple as you walk, making sure you don't begin to rush.

From this exercise you can discover how to take your central balance line, your fulcrum, with you wherever you go, as long as you stay focused on grounding and balancing yourself. Your voice can remain stable as long as this line is unbroken.

CENTERING: THE CORE OF OUR SINGING ENERGY

Having discovered our central balancing *line,* it is now also important to be able to "home in" to our central *point.* This will turn out to be our actual energy source for singing; it is the site of the abdominal and diaphragmatic muscles, which help control the outflow of air. Focusing on it helps us to understand where the voice's power comes from and how to tap into that power.

- Take your grounded stance once more. Put your hands on your belly somewhere just under your naval and close your eyes. Breathe into your belly and feel the inflow of breath push out your hands. Imagine that under your hands is a light bulb that glows brighter as you breathe in. This is the core from which your voice flows. Begin to hum and feel your belly begin to pull in very, very gently toward your spine. Keep your ribcage expanded but not stiff as you draw energy from your belly. Be sure not to let the top half of your body collapse. In your imagination see the bulb begin to dim. When you are almost out of breath, stop humming, and inhale once more. The bulb glows brighter again.

From now on this will be the place from which you draw energy for singing, and with every inhalation, you will imagine topping up your available energy. This central point, the core of your body, is a familiar place to anyone who studies tai chi, yoga, or any martial art. It is the "tan tien," the place from which life energy (chi) flows through the body. If you develop the idea that this is where your singing is initiated, you will strengthen your voice, find you have more control, and decrease unnecessary tensions elsewhere.

Diverting Energy

"Energy itself is neither good nor bad, useful nor harmful, but neutral, since everything depends on the form into which energy passes. Form gives energy its quality...For the creation of real value, both energy and valuable form are needed."
– Carl Jung.

We have only a certain amount of available energy for singing and energy used up in unnecessary places is energy wasted, unavailable for important work in necessary tasks. I've already talked about this in the context of thoughts (mind energy), but we must also apply it to the body. As a singer we must strive to divert misapplied energy (jaw tension, pushing from throat, etc.) to our core, where the important singing "engine" resides. We should see energies as transferable. Thus, if you are trying to sing a high note or phrase by using a lot of muscular tension in the upper body or throat, it probably isn't working very well (or is at least causing some pain). So, instead, transfer that effort to your lower body, demand more of your core energy, and let go of the striving from elsewhere. You may suddenly discover that you reach the high notes with more ease but keep the energy for support in good supply. In the process, you may also discover freer resonance.

As I see it, the "real value" to which Jung refers is, for the singer, the song itself, along with the Authentic Singer's response to and interpretation of it. But, as he says, to create "quality" we need to be concerned also with the "valuable form" (the state of the body) and how the "energy" (the breath) flows into it. There is one important part of our body that holds the whole form together and that is often bypassed when considering the details—the spine.

THE SPINE

Our voices owe an enormous debt to the spinal column. If you have a voice teacher, no doubt you have heard about the importance of keeping a strong spine, and you will have been given exercises for good posture. It is the spine that acts as supporter for the ribs and frees the intercostals for expansion. Grounding, balancing, and centering cannot work without a perfectly aligned spine. If the spine collapses, so does the voice. The breath becomes inhibited and shallow, and the neck muscles tighten, constricting the throat and all the articulator muscles.

The singer must realize the importance not only of keeping the spine strong but also flexible. It is not that we have to take a sergeant major stance with shoulders pressed back and spine locked rigid. That is equally inhibiting to the voice. I have had students who have learned posture either in the armed forces or certain dance classes and have the idea that they must hold themselves stiff as a board. As a consequence, their voices sounded just as locked up. With gentle persuasion, they were able to free the hold on their spine, release their breath, and find much more resonance and vocal beauty.

A strong, flexible spine is also necessary as part of our performance. Collapse the lower spine or neck or allow the shoulders to sag forward and the image you present to your listeners is of either reticence or nonchalance. And if you don't want to be there or don't care about singing for them, why would they ever want to listen? You have lost them before you open your mouth. If, however, you stretch your spine up through each vertebra, and ground, center, and balance yourself, you will feel your voice open up to your demands, and the audience will respond accordingly. So pay close attention to your spine and appreciate its support. Learn to use it to enhance your vocal possibilities and add confidence to your performance.

RAISING YOUR PHYSICAL AWARENESS

Physical bad habits can be extremely difficult to correct and the process of doing so takes time, focus, and awareness. You may need help from someone else to become aware of them. Your voice teacher can certainly help, though you may need to seek out other professionals, depending on the nature and location of your problems. A professional chiropractor could be the person to help with chronic problems of the spine or neck. I also recommend that singers look into studying two or more of the following methods to help them become more physically aware, correct problems, and strengthen important muscle groups:

- Yoga or Tai Chi - wonderful for balance, alignment, body awareness, flexibility, and focus.
- Pilates - helps strengthen the core muscles, which are so important to singing.
- Alexander Technique or Feldenkrais Method - both excellent for body awareness, isolating muscle groups, correcting specific tension issues, balance, and alignment.
- Any martial art - for strength, coordination, focus, and body awareness.

- Many types of dancing can help strengthen core muscles, improve coordination, teach us grounding, and help with balance. Styles that have something special to offer include tango or African dance or even belly dancing!

I also encourage you to use regular aerobic workouts to help develop strength for singing. When I began running, my relationship to my breath changed. Not only did running seem to give me more energy and extend my breath capacity, it also allowed me to keenly observe my breathing and my whole-body connection to it. I watched how, at the beginning of my exertion, my body seemed to panic for fear of lack of oxygen, and I would gasp for air. After a short while, my mind would accept that everything was fine, my body adjusted to the demands on it, and my breathing calmed down to a gentle rhythm. I observed as my body and my mind began to trust my breath. For me, running became a method of meditation and an aid to finding and understanding *flow.*

But whatever practices you add to your routine, always remember your own responsibility in the process because in the end you are the one who must pay attention to correcting posture or loosening tensions or strengthening muscles. No one else will do it for you. Those old habits will jump right back in as soon as you give them a few days' inattention or forget to check up on them regularly. We can so easily be distracted by other vocal problems, musical difficulties, fears, or anxieties. But remember that the smallest physical imbalance or misalignment or inappropriate tension can easily *be the cause* of those things.

Stay physically aware and physically fit.

CHAPTER 8

OUTSIDE THE BOX

OPENING UP TO FLEXIBILITY, CREATIVITY, AND GROWTH

"The real voyage of discovery consists not of seeking new land-scapes but of seeing with new eyes"
– Marcel Proust

Flexibility, creativity, and growth are complementary factors that hold a very important place on our journey to becoming the singer we want to be. Staying flexible to changes in our technique and performance practices leads us to be able to open ourselves to greater creativity, which in turn leads us to expansion of our experiences and growth of our artistic selves.

Some years ago, when I was a visiting coach for a high school girls' choir, I asked the girls to name a favorite singer that they listened to and had seen regularly on video or TV. Hands shot up, and I had a variety of answers: Celine Dion, Nora Jones, Christina Aguilera, Mariah Carey, and Whitney Houston. "Okay," I asked, "Who would like to *be* that star?" Quite a few hands remained aloft. Then I asked who would come out in front of the class and *sing as if they were* that favorite singer? It took a little encouragement, but after some prodding by her friends, Melanie, an obviously extroverted young woman, strutted to the front of the class, already taking on her role. I handed her a large marker pen to simulate a microphone, and she launched into a rendition of "I Will Always Love You," to the whooping and cheering of her friends. After a few bars of a very credible imitation of Whitney Houston, she collapsed in giggles, and the room erupted in laughter all round. "Go on," I said, "You're doing great!" She sang a few more bars, adding gestures and body posturing before breaking down once more in hysterical laughter at herself. I asked for the opinion of her classmates, and everyone agreed that while she was singing she was very good. No one had ever heard her perform like that before.

I asked Melanie if she would like to be a successful singer.

"Yeah, I suppose so...that would be cool," she replied with a nervous giggle.

"So why don't you sing like that and work at becoming one?" I asked.

She looked at me quizzically. "I was just pretending—that isn't how *I* sing!"

I pointed out to Melanie that if she really wanted to sing well, not doing everything she could to do so was a great disservice to herself and to her ambitions. What she had just done was a taste of doing everything she needed to do; she had thrown her full self into being a pop singer, whereas previously she had only ever sung halfheartedly. "But you saw how everyone laughed!" she said.

I understood her problem. The person she had just imitated singing the song with full commitment and great communication was not the person other people expected her to be. It made everyone laugh, including herself, because of the comical juxtaposition of the person she became when she pretended to be someone clsc and the person everyone saw her as. But she and the rest of the girls had glimpsed a new part of Melanie, not someone else. She didn't become Whitney Houston in front of us. She became Melanie, the pop singer.

Melanie learned many different things from her act. She discovered that day that to sing well required much more commitment than she ever realized. In *portraying* a singer she had found part of herself that had not been involved in her singing before—she felt the energy it took, if only for a brief moment, to sing like a pop star. She also came face to face with a person inside her who could BE a very good singer. That young woman had emerged when she had given herself permission to drop her ego—the self by which she defined herself—without being restricted by norms, expectations, and judgments. In a discussion afterward someone in the class said that in pretending to be someone else, Melanie had actually *found* part of herself. There was a lesson to be learned for everyone that day. When we lock ourselves into an old image of ourselves or our voices, or allow other people to lock us into that image, we close the door to improvement and change. We may miss finding the singer we want to be.

Let me make it clear that I am not an advocate of performance by simple imitation. That is not the way to discover our authentic voices or find our unique gift. But by listening to a successful singer, imitating some of the basic *energies* she uses and for a moment *acting as if you are the singer you would like to be*, you may uncover a new part of yourself and add a new dimension to your voice that was trapped behind your past experience. You may find a new way of using your breath or find new colors in your voice or simply discover, as Melanie did, what full commitment feels like.

I heard a young pianist, just launching his professional career, talking about the influence of his famous teacher on his style. He said that imitating someone else's way of playing can only captures the *details* not the *essence* of performance. When you add the essence, that is, your own personal relationship to the music, the performance becomes your own. The essence is for you, the singer, your Authentic Voice, and as I have said, developing that is crucial. But capturing the details is important too and gives us the tools that enable us to expand our possibilities to more truly express that *essence.*

If an artist looks at a painting by Van Gogh and copies it as closely as possible, using the same amount of paint, the thick brush strokes, and the vibrant colors, he will surely learn something new to take to his own painting. But no one will consider his copy an expression of his own art or value it like the original Van Gogh. Copying or mimicking can be a learning tool that leads us to greater understanding of either technique or of ourselves.

Naturally I talk about trying out imitation with the caveat that you do not try copying someone totally inappropriate to your voice type or hurt yourself singing like someone who has no technique and who is probably damaging her own voice! In other words, make sure you choose your model judiciously. Now's the time to listen very carefully to your Adviser.

RISKING CHANGE IN TECHNIQUE

Singers are so lucky. The human voice has innumerable possibilities of variation in sound through the addition or subtraction of undertones and overtones by means of our flexible vocal tract and manipulation of our natural resonances. On any one note we have many choices to make that will affect the way it sounds. No other instrument has such flexibility of color, which is one reason the voice is so adept at transmitting feelings. According to a musician friend of mine, every instrument is yearning to be a human voice. Sadly, we often confine ourselves only within the possibilities that are already familiar to us. Of course it's safer and easier that way. We can be stuck in a box restricted by how we've sung a song before or how we've heard someone else sing it or by fear of what will happen if we try something new.

But if you are not happy with the way your voice sounds or if you simply want to be a better singer, there is only one thing to do. I have already said it and you know it yourself, but it is always worth repeating: *you must change something.* You cannot go on doing exactly what you have been doing and expect it suddenly to go right. You must accept that singing is a risky business and take the risk to change.

YOUR LISTENING EXPERIENCE

"We fail to hear a tone's components largely out of inattention, just as we glance at a tree without noticing its individual branches."
– Robert Jourdain, *Music, the Brain, and Ecstasy*

It goes without saying that we are very familiar with our own voice—or are we? We live with our voice, just as we live with our hands in front of us or the reflection of our face in the mirror. We experience it every day, but are we fully conscious of what it sounds like? What are you noticing when you practice or when you sing? As we have discussed, singing is an immensely complex process. It involves coordinated physical and mental activities to create nuances of sound, color, and pitch. How can we possibly be aware of every aspect of our instrument at once? The answer is we can't. We hear and experience only a part of our voice *at any time*. If we are not paying close enough attention, our tendency is to experience the *same* part each time we sing—the part that we have allowed ourselves to become so very familiar with by constantly focusing on it!

In other words, we have selective hearing when it comes to our own voice, especially when we are listening and singing at the same time. Like most people, when I listen to myself *in a recording,* I am surprised how my performance actually sounds. Of course, we all know there is a difference between the sound we hear from the inside and how it comes across to others listening from the outside. But what I'm talking about here is not something we are incapable of hearing as we sing, but something which is perfectly discernable *if only we'd pay attention.* When I listen carefully enough, I have realized that there are many sounds in my recorded voice that I recognize *from the background* of my own inner tape. In other words, if I'd listened in the right way by opening up my experience and my ears to a broader range of sounds, I could have been better aware of the different qualities in my voice and been more in control of the sound or the pitch. As it was, I was often so focused on a particular aspect of the sound that I missed the experience of the very qualities that I could have utilized to make huge improvements in that performance.

I see it as somewhat like the story of the emperor's new clothes; we are very good at hearing what we want to hear and ignoring what we don't want to hear, even though it may be right there in front of us. Perhaps we block out part of our voice because listening too carefully may expose problems we don't want to deal with. Or perhaps we just become overly familiar and basically stop really *listening* at all.

Many singers will say that they hate listening to themselves sing when confronted with a recording of themselves. This is the ego is at work: "If I'm not perfect I don't want to know it!" But it is vital that we listen to ourselves, live and recorded, if we are to move forward on our journey. Our ears are our most valuable tools for discernment, and singers, more than any musician, have a habit of allowing them to fall into disuse or underuse or sometimes misuse, without even realizing they are doing it. So it's not just a question of listening to ourselves. It's a matter of listening in the right way.

Take vibrato, for example. Often a student with excessive vibrato is not even aware of the problem when she listens to herself practice; she has become so used to her own sound that the vibrato has effectively disappeared from her hearing, gone from the radar like the ultra-high pitches a dog hears that we cannot. But as soon as she hears herself on tape, using "outside listening" to experience her own voice, she becomes aware of the problem and aware of what others hear. Next time she goes into the practice room she will have shifted the way in which she hears herself. Consequently she is able to address the issue because she has learned to listen with "new ears."

The fact is that unless we actively pay attention to all different aspects of our voices we will only notice perhaps a quarter of its potential. We will end up asking only a small part of our total capacity to do the task of our full voice. No wonder we get frustrated!

So bad habits not only manifest themselves in our technique but also can creep into the way we hear our own voice and the way we experience it. Somehow we must give ourselves the opportunity to hear every aspect of our voices to understand it fully and extend our possibilities, as well as find and address the root causes of our vocal problems. Could it be that the answer to many of our singing problems lies right there in our own ears? Eyes or ears, Proust was right. It may not be new "landscapes" we need to seek, just a new way of listening.

CHANGING THE TAPE

At any point on our journey, it is clear that our life is formed by our *past experience.* As we have noted, we are most comfortable with what we have experienced, and familiarity makes us feel safe. But staying stuck in what we already know means we will not be open to change, or, therefore, growth.

It may seem obvious when we are paying someone to teach us or we are reading books like this one that we are not satisfied with the current state of things and want some help to fix problems. But I have had a surprising number of students who come to me to learn but still repeat same thing, expecting to improve. I had one student who never stopped to listen to what I had to say or listen to my demonstrations. He simply jumped right back in to sing the same exercise over again right after I stopped him. I would have to insist on him making eye contact with me and standing still before he would stop fidgeting, concentrate, and listen! His paradigm was his experience with piano lessons. If he made a mistake in piano scales, he simply repeated them over and over until they were right. Repetition was the path to improvement. It took a lot of convincing to have him understand that singing is not like that. Repetition does not necessarily make things right. We have to be fully aware of what we are doing and, if the outcome is not to our liking, do something different next time. *What* to do differently is a matter of listening to our teacher or our Adviser for suggestions, being aware of our own experience, and taking risks with something new.

There is a place for repetition of *good habits* we create for singing. As in any discipline, it is the only way to change the old, bad ones. Yes, practice makes perfect, but only if you practice in the correct way.

How We Practice

Like any musician, a serious singer will have a regular practice routine that usually involves repetition in some form. If you are working on improving your voice, practice is very important; it is the moment to focus on your voice in a conscious way without distractions.

Singers practice in many different ways. One may walk into a room where there is a piano or keyboard and perform a series of vocal warm-ups that usually include slides, hums, and scales before launching into songs or arias. Another may simply sit down with a guitar and start running through songs, repeating some more complex or technically challenging passages. The next may sing along with the radio in an attempt to imitate the latest pop sensation. The efficacy of each of these methods is of course variable and dependent on many factors, though the last method I would suggest is close to useless and hardly to be considered as either practice or serious. However you practice, it is likely that your method has a certain routine to it; you have been taught certain exercises or use certain songs as warm-ups. You cling to these as if they were a life raft, weighing them down with the burden of vocal transformation that you truly believe will happen one day simply because you repeat, repeat, and repeat.

Exercise routines in singing practice certainly have their merits. We need a baseline from which to measure progress. "That exercise/song/note feels much easier today. I'm obviously fixing the tension problem I had." But routine is also a dangerous thing. Falling into singing routines may lead us to:

- Restrict our experience by keeping us within a narrow parameter of exercises. There are, after all, an infinite number of possible aspects to our voice that we must by necessity restrict work on for lack of time per session; so if we also restrict by habit of routine, we do ourselves a serious disservice.
- Allow our ears to fall into a sort of habitual listening that makes them lazy and miss the opportunity to hear new sounds.
- Anticipate an outcome, so we are likely to sing the same way we did yesterday and the day before. Perhaps it wasn't wrong, or even bad, but our *expectation of what the sound will be* also narrows our possibilities and slows our development.
- Avoid our problems by keeping us in a safe, familiar place.

So we need to develop new listening possibilities and changing experiences. How do we do this?

Hearing with New Ears

Let's look at several ways to stimulate your new ears:
- *Change your routine regularly.* Keep one part of your practice the same to have a baseline but constantly create new

exercises and learn new songs. Be imaginative! Practice songs of different styles; begin working on the end of a song first or excerpt the most difficult passages.

- *Put your voice under a microscope by changing the focus of your routine each time you practice.* For instance, choose one particular aspect of your voice, i.e., resonance, articulation, color, vowel shape, or breath flow, or choose a particular area of your voice, i.e., chest voice or head voice, and focus solely on that for the whole practice time or an allotted amount of time. Become minutely aware of all the details of your voice. Try closing your eyes as you practice and don't allow your focus to stray. Then repeat the exercise with your eyes open. Focus on a different aspect each day and then use one day a week to put it all back together. Record yourself that day and try to take your listening outside yourself to get a better idea of the whole.

- *Change where you sing.* Acoustics makes a huge difference and changing them encourages our ears to pay attention! Use a bedroom (usually dull acoustics) one day and a bathroom (highly resonant) the next. Notice how differently your body responds to the changes and pay attention to your own resonance and vibrations.

- *Change the position of your body when you sing.* Try singing while bending over or lying down or kneeling on all fours. Sing while pushing against a wall or leaning up against it with feet angled out at about forty-five degrees, so the spine is supported by the wall. Any or all of these physical alterations may well lead you to new insights into the possibilities of your voice that you otherwise would never experience. I remember when I was singing a leading role in an opera that involved a very difficult passage with a high B, and the director wanted me to sing it leaning over with my head almost upside down. I was amazed when the high B became easier for me to sing!

EXPAND YOUR AWARENESS

even if I have forgotten to listen
Ear is always open
even if in my filtering moments I am not open to receiving
I hear if I remember
I hear more if I remember to remember
I hear if I experience all the vibrations of my body
Vibration is the sole connection to the soul and other souls in the uni-
verse our spiritual musical home.
— Pauline Oliveros, *from "The Earth Worm*
Also Sings", Roots of the Moment

As you make some changes to your routine and your listening habits as I have suggested, your practice will become more spontaneous, and you will open up to new experiences of your voice. Now you must make sure that you utilize its new potential. Now you have to start to listen and feel *with awareness.*

- *Remind yourself to use your ears.* We often have to actually tell ourselves to listen to make our hearing work to its fullest capacity. When you are focusing on breath or tone color or remembering words you may not be listening as attentively as possible. How can you when your brain is focused intently elsewhere? So listening may need to *be* the focus to train your ear to pick up on the details. Also remember that you are "recording" your own sound in your memory each time you sing. The deeper and more focused you listen, the more possibilities you will have to draw on and to pull out of your memory later.

- *Use "outer" ears to listen as if you are the audience.* We hear sound from the outside, as we hear everything around us, and from the inside, picking up vibrations that are coming from the body through the inner ear. When you focus on listening from the outside, you try to put yourself as far away from your sound as possible and take in your voice as a whole, gathering information about the total performance. Record yourself to help you with this. Play the recording and then sing the same passage/song again; hear in your live voice what you heard in the recording. You are teaching yourself to listen, to really *hear your whole voice.*

- *Use your "inner" ears and try to hear details inside the sound.* Begin to do what I call "listening into the corners of your voice." Take time to explore your sound. This can be fascinating. Try this exercise: Sit comfortably, with a well-supported spine, and close your eyes. Breathe deeply into your abdomen a few times. Take a single sound, a hum or any single vowel, and slowly sing "around your voice," first sustaining one pitch and then sliding extremely low or high but always of course with good breath support and a strong spine. Repeat with a different vowel on changing pitches. Keep breathing often and never allow yourself to get too near the end of your breath.
  This is an exploration not a test. Don't do anything that feels uncomfortable or hurts, but take yourself outside of your regular realm of sounds. Make a list of new things you hear. Give yourself permission to sing notes that don't necessarily sound perfect. Make funny noises, open and close resonance spaces, move your tongue around as you sing, change the shape of your lips, feel movement in the soft palate, and use various consonants to familiarize yourself with the possibilities of movement in the articulator muscles. Notice what these shifts do to the sound. Sustain a new sound that sounds interesting, so you familiarize yourself with it; listen all around it. You are discovering new possibilities, maybe new resonances, new colors, and greater range. By using your inner ears you are helping to quiet your Judge and allowing your voice to simply happen. Think of your inner ears as your "authentic" ears, disconnected from your ego and ready to lead you without judgment to your true voice.

- *Be aware not only of listening but of feeling.* As you get more comfortable with the exploration, begin to notice the sensations in your body. Remember your quest is to allow the breath, now transformed into sound waves, to find and utilize resonance. Use your hands to feel for vibrations in your belly, in your chest, and in your cheeks. Sense where you feel vibrations; discover what happens to resonance as you change notes or vowels, or release tensions so you can allow more spaces to vibrate. Do you feel vibration in your chest? Probably, if you are singing low in your range. Your face? Possibly, when you move into your middle register. Your head? Maybe, as you sing higher. Do you still feel the vibrations without touching the places? Does the vibration stay the same when you sing softer? Is there a "buzz" in your sound? If not, can you release some tension and find one? Can you retain and follow this focused vibration in your sound all the way through the dynamic range? (Remember that freeing vibrations is freeing the voice to be more expressive.) Do your lips tingle? If you're humming and relaxed, they probably will. Does your jaw shake? If it does, it's probably because of unnecessary tension that should be released. Is there any pain associated with your singing? I hope not, but if so, address it! If you don't actually feel vibrations, can you *sense* the voice shifting place? Do you have a feeling of where your voice is in your body as you sing a particular note? If not, sing a note as low as you can and then reasonably high to see what sensation your body reports. Play with your sounds, directing them around your body. We can learn so much by listening and feeling what's happening inside.

- *Expand your detailed listening to the world outside of you.* Sit in meditation and settle your mind by focusing on the breath for a few moments. Then take your focus to the outside and listen in detail to the sounds around you. There may be sounds of nature, human sounds, and mechanical or electrical sounds to listen to. Try and distinguish all the sounds you can. You will probably notice the sound of your own breathing, or maybe your heart beating. Make your ears work hard to focus on the sounds, one at a time then all together. Use this once more to bring your attention to the present and avoid letting your mind wander. Make your ears work hard at *listening*.

These are examples of what I call vocal or aural meditations, and they are invaluable for exploring the possibilities in your voice and your senses. You are honing your listening skills and becoming more aware of the work your senses must do to expand your singing experience. Use these exercises also to open up the breathing mechanism, warm up the voice, and focus your mind and body as you prepare for further practice or performance.

LISTENING IN PERFORMANCE

Practicing listening to and feeling our voices only makes the experience of performance that much easier. When we are in the habit of using our ears in practice, we are more likely to be able to use them effectively in performance, when we rely on them for discernment of pitch, color, and sound when acoustics are unfamiliar. By practicing in this way, you create flexibility to deal with all sorts of situations. Having thoroughly explored your sound, you are less likely to take yourself by surprise in performance and have many more possibilities to take on stage with you to have at your command.

But be aware that listening as intently as I've talked about so far in this chapter takes somewhat of a backseat in performance, since this sort of listening is about detail and not the whole picture. When we get into performance, we have to let the right brain take over and let the performance flow rather than be too concerned with detail. We are now in the mode of communicating not just listening. Keep your ears aware and alert but don't let them take away your first responsibility of giving a good overall performance. Since we can only truly focus on one thing at a time, we will not be fully engaged with our song or our audience if we are only listening to ourselves.

Over-listening in performance can, in fact, become a problem. So concerned are we on how we sound that we start what I call "listening backwards." By this I mean our ears become focused on how the last note or phrase *sounded* and not on what we are currently doing. (This sometimes happens in practice or voice lessons too.) This can lead to all sorts of issues, including inattention to communication of the song, slowing of the tempo, lack of anticipation of what is coming up, and memory slips. So too much listening can actually get in the way of an effective performance. As detailed in chapter 4, your focus must now stay on your Gift: the music, the words, and your communication with your listeners. If a few sounds emerge that are not entirely to your liking, you must instantly leave them behind and not allow them to distract you. The same goes for a *beautiful* note you may have sung, which can be just as distracting. So, in performance, relax your efforts at listening and let things flow. Now is the time for your listeners to use *their* ears and enjoy the experience!

CREATIVITY AND INSPIRATION

The next step on our singing journey is to open ourselves up to creativity and inspiration.

It is easy to overlook the creative side of a singer's life. Performers are often looked on as conduits for the flow of other people's creativity (the composer and poet/lyricist), not as creative animals themselves. But creativity must be a part of all aspects of our singing.

It seems evident to me that once a song is written, the performer is the only dynamically creative force; how the song sounds is entirely determined by the individual interpretation, sound, and personality of the singer. So the singer's influence is indeed great, and it will be his own personal vision of a song that will allow a listener to have a new experience. It is important to remind yourself to develop that vision. After all, your vision and voice are unique to you, and create your mark on the song and a whole new experience for your audience. If we perform by merely imitating or by simply trying to sing exactly what we see written on the sheet of music, we deny our full commitment to sharing ourselves with our listeners and deny our creativity as performers. There are mere imitators in every genre of music, and an audience may well be taken in by the amazing skill of imitation. However, imitation is the safe path and will not lead either you or your listeners to moments of inspiration or joy.

We see examples of the creative power of the performer in all styles of music. It is perhaps most clearly evident in a style such as jazz, where improvisation around a melody and new interpretation is valued and expected as part of the genre. Compare Ella Fitzgerald's version of "My Funny Valentine" with Shirley Horn's, and you hear how Rodgers and Hart, the song's composers, almost disappear behind the performers' distinctive interpretations of their song. The same happens in cover versions of pop songs; Whitney Houston's performance of "I Will Always Love You" is entirely different from Dolly Parton's, the song's writer. Adam Lambert stunned the *American Idol* audience with his rendition of Johnny Cash's "Ring of Fire." Despite the contrast in styles, each performance is successful in its own right; the listener gains new insight with every singer's interpretation because he is touched by each singer's unique life experience through which the song if filtered.

Even in classical music where there is an underlying assumption that the singer must be exactly true to the rhythms and notes on the page, where our inhibitions are naturally the greatest, there is still room for flexibility, creativity, and imagination. For example, I have three recordings of a particular English art song, one by Janet Baker, a mezzo-soprano, one by Ian Bostridge, a tenor, and one by Bryn Terfel, a bass-baritone. I am amazed at the beauty of each and the difference in the interpretations. Yet all the performances are moving renditions because each is true to the Authentic Voice of the singer. So even though in classical music one doesn't have free rein to rewrite notes and change rhythms arbitrarily, the intention of the song, its meaning, the words themselves, and the expression of the singer's own response to it, is still paramount. If that means an almost imperceptible holding back or emphasis on a word here or quickening through a phrase there, it is vital to do just that. There are of course bounds of taste and style to be taken into consideration, but usually, if you know the music and the style well enough, your Adviser will let you know when you've crossed those bounds (assuming you are still listening). A successful performance of any song, then, will be one where the singer adds her own imagination to that of the song creators.

FINDING INSPIRATION

"Inspiration may be a form of superconsciousness or perhaps of sub-consciousness—I wouldn't know. But I am sure that it is the antithesis of self-consciousness."
>   – Aaron Copland, *composer*

Inspiration is, by definition, a sudden happening, a flash, a eureka moment that can leap out at us at any time. Such moments in singing may occur when we transform something we've understood intellectually into something we actually experience in our bodies, or when we allow ourselves to let go of old, safe habits and open up new possibilities by taking a quantum leap into the unknown. The opportunity for inspiration is created by making choices and releasing control of the outcome.

I had a young student who came to me wanting to sing country music just like Garth Brooks. It was the music he listened to all the time and, in his limited experience, the only music he liked. He played guitar very well and impressed me with the conviction and sincerity with which he sang. But he was having trouble with his upper range and tensions in his middle voice that distorted the words and made his listeners somewhat uncomfortable.

We worked on his voice technically and began to address some of his issues but weren't ironing out all the problems. So I suggested that we work on some classical Italian arias, then a musical theater song, genres so unfamiliar to him I thought he might resist. But he was prepared to risk leaping into the unknown and rose to the challenge eagerly. He learned songs with a wider range than he had ever attempted and some were even in an unfamiliar language. As I led him through this new territory, old habits began to slowly disappear. His voice became freer, his range improved dramatically, and he found he was having a lot of fun with his new discoveries; he was learning not only how to use his voice better but also understanding how interesting and beautiful other styles of music could be. His ah-ha moment was when he realized he really liked his voice singing these totally new styles and that maybe he had something to offer that even

Garth Brooks didn't have! Suddenly, a new world of experience had opened up to him as a performer and listener. Now he could take his technical improvements and his broader musical and personal experience, and apply them to his country music, with the result that his whole performance was deeper and even more committed—you might even say *inspired.*

STAYING AWARE

Above all, it is imperative to stay aware. If we are not alert and on the lookout for inspiration it may pass us by, and our opportunity for growth will be gone. Like everything else, staying present in the moment, focused, and aware is the surest way to nurture this vital aspect in the development of our singing.

You will discover that you open doors to your creativity and inspiration as you begin to take control of your monkey brain and explore your voice through the practice of just a few minutes' meditation a day as suggested in chapter 4. Quieting your mind sweeps away the clutter of thoughts that may be obscuring the revelations you seek. Use the vocal/aural meditation exercises I suggested earlier in this chapter to help you develop your creative instincts. This approach may be applied to a particular song or to developing a new direction in your singing career or to solving a nagging technical problem you've struggled with for so long. Creativity and inspiration are essential parts of the singer's tool kit, and you must not underestimate their value nor let them stagnate. Pay attention to using your creative mind in each part of the singing process.

ENCOURAGING YOUR CREATIVE MIND IN PRACTICE AND PERFORMANCE:

- *As you practice or in voice lessons stay conscious not self-conscious.* As I said earlier, singing practice involves its share of repetition, but it is also about *allowing* moments of revelation and inspiration to happen. In this process we must take to heart Copland's words. We cannot afford to be self-conscious about our singing if we hope for inspiration. Only by pushing the ego (the Judge) out of the way and keenly observing will our revelations come. Be on the lookout for that slight change of sensation or sound that will lead you, if you pursue it, to a whole new freedom for your voice. Listen carefully to both your singing voice and the voice of your Adviser. Observe your body and "listen" to what it tells you, too. The learning moments can easily pass you by if you are not present in your practice all the time or if you only hear what you expect to hear and feel what you have always felt. There are layers to the voice—mixtures of resonances, emotional involvement, physical exertion—that can obscure each other unless you are paying close attention and staying open to something new appearing. In voice lessons, be conscious of allowing your teacher to guide you to these new experiences. By watching, feeling, and experiencing without judgment, you will *discern* when that something new is right.

- *Take time to rest.* Just as a marathon runner cannot simply run every single day and hope for progress, so I believe we singers must give ourselves regular time off for recharging our batteries. I advise perhaps one day every week or two without singing at all and a whole week's break every six months or so. It is particularly interesting to observe your voice carefully after you've rested it for a while. New things may happen spontaneously because for a precious few moments the old habits may be caught off-guard, sluggish from their rest. This can be a time for great revelation. Allow your voice to find its own way, give it chance to show what it can do when you are not trying so hard to steer it where it has always gone. Release control and just observe. You may like what you hear and feel. Of course, it takes a keen observer to stay with the new feelings and not allow the habitual problems to re-emerge, but simply being aware may help you to capture some benefit and experience a new approach to an old problem. You may have broken through a barrier that was inhibiting your progress. The task now is to identify what you are doing—or not doing—to have allowed the change to happen.

- *Use visualization in technique.* Most voice teachers have favorite images to give you to help in the understanding and application of technique. You may have heard 'the chimney through the head,' 'ping pong ball on a fountain (or hair-dryer),' 'egg on the tongue,' 'flowing stream,' 'old-man-asleep-in-the-chair jaw,' or many more. Hopefully, you are able to distinguish between the ones that help you and the ones which don't. It will certainly be a personal thing. Remember that you can also create your own images, especially if the ones your teacher suggests just don't create the right effect for you. So take the various images and look at what your teacher is trying to help you to do. 'Old-man-asleep-in-the-chair' is obviously an aid to imagining what a relaxed jaw might feel like. Find alternative images which will produce the same effect. 'Valley Girl jaw' might do the trick for some (duh!). 'Bored Valley Girl' might work even better and get your throat open (yawning) at the same time! Use your imagination. Don't blame your teacher for your lack of response to their image. Look for the result your teacher is after and be actively involved in your own progress.

- *Do not to be inhibited by the look of the notes/rhythm on the page.* It is important to understand that the system of musical notation a composer is working with is severely limited. It is always only an approximation of what he has in his head, so it is up to you to be creative when reading music and interpreting what must become *your* song. The composer (if that isn't you) has put down his pen and handed the piece over to you, the performer. The composer trusts that you will understand that what he's written is as close as he can come to conveying what he wants and that you now have the responsibility to add your humanity to the song, bringing it to life as he cannot do. That is your job. And it entails staying flexible about what you are looking at (the notes) and allowing your feeling, body, and Authentic Voice to come through to give the song its dynamic power.

- *Don't get locked into someone else's interpretation and sound.* If you are a singer who sings for the most part by ear, from listening to other performers alone, you have different problems. In your ear is the way someone else sings the song. So, to make the song your own, you must consciously allow yourself the freedom to do different things and use different colors. Use others' performances only as a guide when necessary or a jumping off point for your own inspiration about a piece.

- *Use your imagination and creativity to find meaning beyond the definitions of the words you are singing.* Search for your own connection to the words and their meaning; imagine you had written the words and describe to yourself what they mean to you personally. Create a story around the text with you at the center. Be the subject or the narrator. Write down whole scenarios and get a strong overview of the song so that you see it as a picture in front of you. Use your meditation skills to focus your mind on your song; sit comfortably, close your eyes, and take three deep breaths. Now visualize scenes where you might be as you are singing the words of your song or what you are looking at as you sing them. Change the setting if necessary until you really feel comfortable with your images. Practice singing your song as you sit focused on the images you create. Sense what story or picture feels the most real to you and use that as the basis of your visualization when you practice performing or when you actually perform. If you see these pictures and bring the song to life for yourself as you perform, the audience will see them, too, and begin to feel what you feel.

- *Keep your breath involved in the process.* Remind yourself that the way you use your breath reflects what you and the character you have created who is singing the song feel. It must carry with it the quality of the emotions of the song; it is never detached. Allow your breath to change its quality to help you create the picture and the deep experience of the song for your audience.

If you stay on the familiar path, the fascinating new experiences that await you will remain hidden, and you'll never know what they could be. Allow yourself to go exploring. Give yourself new possibilities. Use your imagination. Open up a new world and leap into the unknown. Then maybe you will discover a world far more satisfying, more wonderful, than the one you have locked yourself into until now.

Open up to your senses. Stay flexible and stay creative.

CHAPTER 9

THE HIGH WIRE ACT

MAINTAINING BALANCE

"There is no energy unless there is a tension of opposites...
Life is born only of the spark of opposites."
– Carl Jung

So far in this book, I have been encouraging you to dig deep and fully commit yourself to discover the singer you want to be. Now I have to ask you to take a step back and understand the very important role of balance in the art or the *heart* of singing.

There are two aspects of balance to become aware of:
- The Goldilocks syndrome - not too hot, not too cold but *just right.*

When we feel ourselves beginning to try too hard or when fear prevents us from committing ourselves fully, we need to seek balance from a Goldilocks standpoint. It is so easy for each of us to lose our sense of "just right" when we are seeking approval from the outside or give in to our fears instead of trusting our Adviser.
- The principle of yin and yang - balancing one concept with its opposite.

If we have a tendency to become narrowly focused on one aspect of our singing and blinker ourselves to the problems that such a narrow focus can create, we need to remind ourselves of yin and yang, and the necessity for the "tension of opposites."

In either situation the key is to open yourself up to listening to your inner voice, that is the Adviser, not the Judge. When you do, suddenly you realize that you know much more than you thought about the right *balance* in your singing.

Let's look at the role of balance in the light of some of the topics we've discussed so far.

BALANCE OF POWER AND HUMILITY

In leading you to acknowledge the power in your voice and through singing, I do not mean to lead you away from *humility*. As we have seen, singing can have a tremendous impact on lives in many diverse circumstances, but we must always keep it in the context of the whole. In other words, singing is only a small part of the rich tapestry of arts and experiences in the world that go together to enrich all our lives. If we remind ourselves of the place singing has within the whole, we resist elevating our status in the world to feed the ego and keep our sense of power balanced with humility. Our society's tendency to elevate pop stars to near-deity status doesn't help this balance. In fact, in this sort of hero worship—the very ego feeding I have been talking about—we find the seeds of destruction for any singer. It is no wonder we hear so often of the downfall or even death of yet another star to drugs or alcohol. It is far too easy for the voice of our Adviser, our humility, to be lost beneath the cacophony of the demands of the power-hungry ego.

BALANCING THE EGO AND THE AUTHENTIC SELF

I have talked a lot about finding your authentic voice, listening to the Adviser, and quieting the ego, the Controller. But for most of us, unless we become Buddha-like or Christ-like and achieve an enlightened state (which I very much wish for you all, by the way), the ego is here to stay. Indeed, it is inseparable from the authentic self like the head and tail of a coin. We could even argue that a singer *must* have a developed sense of ego to be successful. My emphasis in chapter 2 on listening to and expressing oneself through the Authentic Singer within comes from my experience that it is this voice that is most easily over-

looked and often gets completely buried under the more dominant ego, creating an imbalance that leads us down a dangerous path determined by the insecurities of the Diva or Introvert.
Balancing ego-consciousness with the authentic self is really what
it's about. So what I suggest is that we come to understand when
the ego has a place in our singing and how it can work to our
advantage.

PUTTING THE EGO IN ITS PLACE

There are times when the ego is *constructive* and times when
it is *destructive.* The difference is *at what stage of the process* the ego
emerges and how much power it is given to lead your thoughts
once it manifests itself.

Consider these situations:

Situation number one: You have just given a very good performance for an especially appreciative audience. The ego voice in
your head says:

- Constructive: "I loved the feeling of gratitude and love I
  felt from my audience when I shared that beautiful song
  with them. I want more of that feeling."
- Destructive: "I only want to sing if my audience is going
  to respond as they did today, be grateful for all the hard
  work I put in and value my talents. I want them to show
  me how much they appreciate me because otherwise it's
  not worth it."

In this scenario, the *constructive* emergence of the ego is
directly *after* the performance itself. To experience euphoria over
one's success and enjoy the accolades once the Authentic Singer
has sung is only going to energize you for the next performance.
However, the *destructive* thought may follow directly on from the
first if the ego is allowed to dominate. It becomes greedy and
yearns for the feeling this performance has given it. If the ego
takes control at this point, in an instant it will override the original reason for success of the performance—the emergence of

your Authentic Singer, as we've already discussed. Then it will take you on the path of failure. If you allow this to happen, at the next performance your *intention* will be to gain the approval of the audience to satisfy your craving ego, not to provide enrichment in the form of your song. The ego's demands and expectations become priority and set up the all-too-familiar barrier between performer and audience. You begin to be driven by the *wrong intention.* It is easy to see that this sort of situation could easily arise for a singer thrust into the public eye and whose fame becomes a big distraction from the original *intention.* Suddenly focus is on what the singer will get from the audience and not on what he will give to them.

Situation number two: You are struggling with a technical problem in your voice

- Constructive: "I feel really good about myself when I focus in on problems I'm having and find a way to solve them. I know I am capable of changing this for the better."
- Destructive: "I'm stupid because I can't solve this problem. Here I am spending a fortune on a voice teacher, and I still don't understand what I'm doing wrong. I must be worthless as a singer and shouldn't be doing this."

Here the constructive ego has its place *outside* the problem solving process not *in* it. If the ego jumps into the *process*, the judge and jury come right along to block the clear path to the solution and lead directly to the destructive thought of failure. If you are clever enough to solve the problem yourself, let the ego in *once you've solved it.* It's fine to feel good about yourself and pat yourself on the back for a job well done. It's also fine to have faith that you will be clever enough to solve the problem. But don't even open the door a chink to the greedy ego while you are in the middle of tackling the problem and feeling very vulnerable.

A better approach would be to listen to the Adviser first:

"If I can't solve this problem, I'll have to look for help. I've tried all the things I know to make this work, but I'm not finding the answer. Perhaps someone can help me."

Then later feel free to give your ego a well-deserved boost:

"What a great idea it was to give that teacher/book/class a try because it helped me so much."

Of course there can be times on our singing path when the gap between recognizing a problem and actually fixing it can be very wide. I know from experience that some vocal or psychological issues around singing can take a very long time to resolve. It may feel like you will never find the solution or an easier path. This makes keeping the impatient ego out of it all the more difficult. My advice in this case is to keep letting go of your obsession with the specific problem to work on other aspects of your singing and coming back to it once in a while, each time looking to see if there is another approach to take to solve it. At the same time, keep reminding yourself that perfection is relative and where you are now is not wrong or imperfect. You may find that by adopting this approach the problem actually works itself out. The demanding ego, always expecting so much and always so ready to judge your failure, has probably been the very obstacle in your path all the time!

By *objectifying* the ego like this and treating it as separate from you, the Authentic Singer, you can begin to step back and observe its strong influence and stay in control of its destructive side while feeding on its constructive, positive aspects. In this way you balance it with your authentic voice and take another step closer to becoming the singer you want to be.

FACING THE FEAR OF COMMITMENT: FINDING A SAFETY NET

In chapter 3, I encouraged you to commit to your performing task by immersing yourself in the song and holding nothing back from your audience—an aspect of performance that can fill us with dread. We are fearful enough in everyday life of exposing our emotional selves to our closest friends and relatives, so why would we find it easy or even possible to do so in public to an audience of strangers? My answer to this is that we have a cushion and a safety net—our song. Though we pour ourselves and our emotions into our singing, it really is the *song* itself we are sharing with people.

We have to tell the truth, the whole truth, and nothing but the truth of what we feel about the song and not hide that or obfuscate it with self-consciousness. But, as I once heard a young performer say, we are the pizza delivery boy not the pizza. No one cares much about the delivery boy as long as the pizza tastes good. Our song is what matters, and we should not get so tied up in self-importance to negate that. The song may *convey* our truth, but it is *separate* from us. To balance your view of performing, remember that the song will be the cushion or filter between you and that fearsome audience. Through the filter, they don't look so scary after all. Understand that your audience is there to experience your *song* not *you personally*[11]. Afterward you will bask in the glow of having delivered the best "pizza" anyone ever experienced!

BALANCE AND THE BRAIN

As well as housing the Controller and the Adviser (the ego and the authentic self), the left and right hemispheres of the brain have other functions. The left brain concerns itself with details, problem solving, analysis, technique, and *control*; the right brain takes care of the whole, the big picture, emotions, ideas, and *allowing*. We have emphasized the need to develop right-brain activities to help you become the singer you want to be because that is most often the side that is neglected. But in fact the two sides must come together in perfect equilibrium if we are to sing well.

In practice or in the studio, we are likely to find the left brain dominant. We study and try to understand our voices in great detail. In voice lessons you will recognize the terminology of *balance* in technique: typical images voice teachers might use are the archer pulling back on the bow (opening up the pharyngeal cavity) to let the arrow (the breath) free to fly forward to its target (the resonance) or holding on to the string of a kite (anchoring the larynx and staying grounded) to allow the kite (breath/

---

11   I really believe that this is true even for superstars who appear to be virtually worshipped by fans. It is, after all, the music that moves those fans in the first place and the reverence shown the performer only exists because of that. The fact that superstardom can subsequently take on a life of its own does not negate this.

voice) to soar freely to the sky (high notes) or simply think up as you move down or think down as you move up images. These images provide vital directions from the brain to encourage the correct physical responses to make singing easier.

But at a certain moment, particularly in performance, or when we practice performance, we simplify, step back from our analysis and begin to let our instincts and our overall feeling for the music take over. We open our singing to that right-brain character, our Adviser. We just sing with a particular song in mind, unencumbered by outside thoughts, fully *in flow*. If we can do this, then all the details we've studied happen through us instinctively, and the picture comes perfectly into focus for us and our listeners. Of course, the key is to have worked through the details enough to create the right *instincts* in performance and to be sure to have erased our old bad *habits* that will trip us up before we even get to *flow*. Remember that habits are not synonymous with instincts. Instincts come from the authentic self and may guide us to *good* habits in our singing, but *bad* habits can easily be created by the needs of the ego. As I've already stressed, these can divert us way off our singing path and tie us in "bad habit knots."

I have noticed that many of my students can work out technical problems in exercises perfectly well, but it becomes all too predictable that as soon as they begin to sing a song, the old bad habits kick right back in. Expecting instant transformation, they forget they have to work to apply what we have discovered *to each song*. Never underestimate the patience and work involved in breaking old habits and grounding yourself in the good ones. But at a certain moment, as you practice, look out for the moment when you can finally trust your newly honed instincts and let go of your detailed analysis and blow-by-blow commentary. Give your right brain the chance to take over the driver's seat as you develop your performance. *Allow* yourself simply to sing.

Maintaining Emotional Balance

If we are not emotionally involved in what we sing and do not allow ourselves to communicate an emotional connection to our audience, our performance will fall flat. We must sing songs that mean something to us, and that we care enough about to want to share them with others. Only then does our Authentic Singer find its voice.

But imagine a song that moves us to tears. How can we fully commit ourselves without choking up and compromising our performance? We have to find emotional balance. This is a choice we make and does not mean we don't fully "feel" the song or somehow compromise the depth of feeling we portray. On the contrary, we free ourselves to communicate our responses clearly. We *tell the story* of our pain rather than being overwhelmed by it. In doing so we set up the balance to allow our listener to feel safe to fully feel the emotions *we* first encountered. Our listeners may weep buckets of tears, but we keep our composure. Our goal is to allow our *audience* to feel—not to show off how much *we* feel. As the writer and director Noel Katz once said "It's all about the audience. We don't care if *you* feel it, *we've* got to feel it—we, the audience."

Many of my students ask how to do this. "But I can't even begin to sing that song without crying!" My approach is to begin by fully immersing ourselves in our feelings *before* we perform and come through to the other side of them. Imagine a stand-up comedian coming across a hilarious joke for the first time. He falls on the floor laughing, unable to speak through his tears of laughter. If he puts the joke into his routine, it would be hopeless if his response each time he told the joke were the same. A comedian mostly wants to remain poker-faced for greatest effect on his audience. So what is his solution? To become so familiar with the joke that he goes through his laughter, and though he still *sees* how funny it is, it no longer has the same physical effect on him.

The same goes for the singer. I would like to share an experience I had that led me to understand what we have to do to avoid the dreaded choking up in performance. When I was planning my wedding to my husband, Bruce, I decided my greatest gift to him would be to write him a song and sing it for him at our reception. I wrote it over several weeks and because it touched on so many very personal things, I cried as I was writing it and cried as I was practicing it. It got to the point that I could hardly think about it without choking up. But I realized that if I were to perform it for him, I had to face my own emotions. I had to keep singing it, thinking about, and working on it until I became at peace with it. After all, like weddings themselves, it wasn't exactly sad—it was full of joy and hope and love and everything one expects of a wedding song. But just like weddings themselves, it had the effect of drawing tears. So I gave my song what it needed: time, work, and thought.

The time element was simply a matter of spending several minutes of each day with my song. The more familiar with it I became, the easier it became to step away from it and look at it objectively, without becoming completely detached. I was simply allowing myself to progress through my emotions. The work needed was in the form of studying the song in detail: ironing out any technical problems, memorizing the words, and generally getting to know every corner of it. I was making sure my body was programmed perfectly to sing the song on autopilot if necessary. I put my mind to work observing my own emotional reactions, which could appear in different places every time I sang my song, and working out what thoughts were triggering them. I would also imagine my listeners (particularly my husband, of course) and visualize their reactions as I was performing my song. Using detailed work and lots of imagination, I was able to anticipate and therefore prepare myself for my own and others' response to the song.

By the time the day came, I knew exactly how I wanted it to sound and how to set it up for greatest effect on my audience. I pulled it off without a tear from me but plenty from my listeners, including, of course, my new husband! It had all been a lesson in how to balance feeling a song fully but not allowing those feelings to get in the way of the audience's emotional experience of the performance of it.

So, whether it's a hilarious comedy number or a devastatingly sad song, we must allow ourselves to work *through* the emotion to the other side. I would even say here that the *deeper* you can delve into those emotions while looking at why you react as you do, the more moving your performance will be and the less likely your technique will be compromised. You will have worked through your reactions, understood them, cried your tears, laughed your laughs, and moved on to a place where you can share it with your listeners.

Of course, this means going the whole way in practice and not holding back because no one is there to see you (though the Diva will be disappointed not to have an audience) or withholding because of self-consciousness (as the Introvert would naturally prefer). So here we are looking once more at an aspect of *commitment* in practice and performance and of setting aside the ego in favor of the authentic self. All on our way to attaining *balance*.

BALANCE OF CONSCIOUS AND INTUITIVE CONTROL

In chapter 3 we discussed how in every style of singing there always has to be commitment to both technique and emotional expression to be truly successful. The opera star singing complex coloratura[12] will lose her audience's attention if she withdraws her emotional involvement; a rock singer will quickly lose his voice if he doesn't support his emotional outbursts with sound technique. So it is not a question only of *committing* yourself to both sides but of *balancing* the emotional and technical sides of a performance. You may recognize an imbalance in some singers who are extremely competent technically but don't move their audience because they are too wrapped up in simply making sure their technique works to convey much emotion. Or you may have been in a situation where you became so emotional about a song you lost all technical control. The greatest performers know what a difference the careful balance of these two elements can make. When you find the right balance, the control you have over your whole performance and your satisfaction in it will be hugely enhanced.

The reason this balance is so difficult to achieve is what is at its root: *control* (manifested by technique) and *letting go of control* (giving in to emotional expression). The scariest thing for a singer or anyone is to let go of control. Yet, as we have discussed, the only way forward on our journey is to do something different, to relinquish certainty, and to take risks.

---

12   Coloratura is the florid embellishment or ornamentation of a vocal line in classical singing, usually involving rapid, running passages across a broad vocal range.

This is where our Adviser comes in. At the point we feel we are letting go of control we should in fact be handing over to our Adviser. If we could trust that this benevolent character will always be there to gently guide us rather than screaming for familiarity and power like the Controller, we wouldn't feel as if we were giving up control at all. As we do this and really begin to trust *ourselves,* we find we can express ourselves freely without fear and still retain technical security.

The ancient Taoists had a name for this concept. They called it *wu-wei,* a state of effortless effort, where we feel alert, focused, and receptive while allowing ourselves to be carried along by the energy of whatever task we are performing. When we get to this place in our singing, it can feel as if the song virtually sings itself. This is control or effort led by intuition and present moment awareness.

The opposite of this is control led by thought, based on history and expectation, and driven by a specific goal. This type of control subverts spontaneity, puts a lock on our imagination, and, most importantly, alienates an audience if it is perceived. *No listener wants to see your effort.* As I have already said, you, the performer, should essentially be evident only as the conveyor of the song. But there are times in our performance when this type of conscious control is necessary to negotiate extremely technically difficult passages, for instance, or remind ourselves of a specific action required for success.

So we need to find a balance between these two types of control in our singing, using intuitive control most of the time in performance, but allowing conscious control to kick in when a problem arises that needs to be solved immediately or when a difficult passage needs to be negotiated. What we must seek is to allow our intuitive control to take the lead most of the time, putting conscious control in the background for momentary use only. With this balance, we are much more likely to create those moments of inspiration that distinguish great from good.

When we use just the right amount of focused energy, set the whole voice into perfect "motion" (vibration), and all parts are in equilibrium, then the "effort" it takes to make that happen feels "effortless." Suddenly it all feels so simple and so easy. The sense of strain or hard work simply disappears. Any singer who has experienced this knows the joy of that feeling.

We come back to what I talked about in chapter 6, regarding the breath: we must allow things to happen while staying completely aware of gentle direction of our action by thought or minor physical adjustments. The more we can let go of too much effort or forcing the outcome by conscious control and allowing intuitive control to guide us, the more certain we become of the outcome. We begin to *trust* rather than *control*. We end up guiding the *whole* but allow the *details* to take care of themselves.

Do not think that letting go of conscious control in performance, however, means giving up on the work we must do to find our way to the intuitive control I'm talking about. It is vital to keep stepping observantly along our path, fixing problems as they arise, and patiently working out the glitches. Only then will we be able to put together the puzzle of our voices and discover the wonderful calm at the center of our singing "storm." The powerful energy all around will then be ready to sweep up our audience, while we remain perfectly in balance at the center, gently guiding the action.

GOLDILOCKS IN THE VOICE STUDIO

I have found that my students tend to fall into three categories:

- Those who listen attentively and apply what I say by doing it in an excessively exaggerated manner.
- Those who listen attentively and think they are applying what I suggest but actually just keep doing the same things they've always done.
- Those who listen attentively, process what I've suggested, try it out, and sense whether it helps by referring to their own Adviser.

You might say it's exactly the Goldilocks scenario: too hot, too cold, or just right.

The reason for each one of these responses is no doubt rooted in the singer's personality. The too-hot student is undoubtedly looking for approval and affirmation from me or is a subscriber to the more-is-always-better philosophy. This student also undoubtedly has little trust in her Adviser or can't even hear its voice over the cacophony of the ego's demands. The too-cold student is probably struggling with fear of change, risk, or the unknown. My just-right students have figured out the balance of listening to the teacher, trying new things, and listening to the reaction of their bodies and Advisers. Approaching voice lessons or any learning experience in this way allows these students to reach their goals quicker and opens the door for the all-important revelations on their singing path.

You may see that the dominance of the Diva or the Introvert is what is inhibiting some of my students from truly discovering the easiest and most productive path forward on their quest to become the singer they want to be.

GIVE AND TAKE: A BALANCE BETWEEN YOU AND YOUR AUDIENCE

"Involve the audience as a fellow player; together hand in hand… An audience is neither refreshed, nor entertained (nor inspired) when not included."

– Viola Spolin, *Improvisation for the Theater*

I believe singing is an autotelic experience. That is, it can be enjoyed for its own sake: if we want it to be, it can be its own end, its own goal. As we have seen, we can achieve high levels of satisfaction—happiness—from the act of singing alone when singing is connected to our authentic self.

But the singer's journey is usually not a one way highway. We can all enjoy singing in the shower or with the radio or while practicing, but, as with many things in life, an even greater benefit is gained from sharing our experience and connecting with others. Whether as a solo performer or member of a choir, an added dimension is discovered when the singing experience is enjoyed by a listener.

Think of a performance situation. A symbiotic relationship is set up between singer and audience. If the performer is singing from his authentic self—without constraint, taking risks, truly expressing himself and his feelings through the song—the listener is freed to explore the same authentic emotions within herself. A trust is set up, which is sensed on both sides, and a cyclical connection created. The deeper the singer goes, the deeper the listener feels comfortable to go, the more risks the singer feels comfortable to take, the deeper he reaches inside himself, the more the listener feels she gets out of the singer, the happier everyone feels, and so it goes on.

However, if the singing is not authentically based, the listener senses a withholding which makes her uncomfortable and leads to signals of discomfort being sent back to the performer; this is interpreted by the singer as a lack of trust or negative judgment which in turn deepens the unwillingness of the singer to fully share himself and reflects back to the listener once more as inauthentic. Thus the opposite, negative cycle is created.

In order to set up the positive cycle of giving and taking it is important to begin with recognition of the cycle.

SHARING YOUR GIFT: LETTING YOUR LISTENER HELP

I mentioned in chapter 1 that I see singing as empathic. But authentic singing only *begins* with the idea of wanting to share an experience with the listener. That is the seed of success. To allow it to grow and blossom, the singer must open himself up to receiving something back from the listener. As the singer opens his heart to the audience, if all is going well, the audience members will open themselves to the gift, and an energy that feels like support or encouragement flows back to the performer. To make this cycle work, the singer must be open to accepting this flow of positive energy and the audience must feel this receptivity.

Problems arise when instead of accepting the listeners' presence and embracing the support they have to offer, the singer looks out as if into a mirror and sees only himself. This may well sometimes feel like the safest thing to do. After all, an audience can be very scary, so why not pretend they aren't there? I've even heard a teacher suggest that we see the audience as a herd of cows in order not to have to deal with the idea of real people out there! But in doing this, the performer ends up singing only for himself. From his own listener's ego he will receive either judgment and criticism or self-aggrandizement and preening. Both of which create a barrier to the audience who then feel cut out of the communication path and disconnected from the authentic message.

Recognize that it is when we sing with our ego in the way, as the flaunting, needy Diva or the bashful, withholding Introvert, that we emphasize our separation from others. What we so crave as human beings, however, is connection to others. Singing is a perfect pathway to that connection, if only we can break through the ego barrier and sing as the Authentic Singer. This way the path between singer and listener is clear to allow unhindered communication. The singer and listener are enveloped and united by the song.

The key is not to see performance as an active/passive situation—the performer performs and the audience listens. That is to deny the real energy a listener has to contribute. Any performer will tell you that the sense of success of a performance is so often determined by the response obtained from their listeners. If the singer acknowledges and receives the reciprocal energy from the listeners, a balance of contribution between the two parties is created. Everyone feels involved in the process. When a person talks of having the audience "in the palm of my hand," this is what is happening; the singer sets up an experience for the listeners, the audience responds, the singer intensifies his emotional commitment, and so it goes on. Only when a singer recognizes this possibility and grants the listeners power without being afraid of the consequences can this successful performance experience happen.

Another consequence of seeing the audience as allies and sharing in our performance is that our fear of them diminishes and in the process the fight-or-flight instinct simply evaporates. We no longer want to run away because our fear is transformed into the excitement of possibility.

So, however lonely or isolated singing, particularly solo singing, might feel, you really are not alone when you stand up on stage. And more often than not your companion in the task (the audience) is willing to send you all the love and support you need to do your very best. In fact, I believe our listeners have it in their power to help free our Authentic Voice. Open yourself to their support and you will discover your task is not so difficult.

> *"Music fills the infinite between two souls."*
> – Rabindranath Tagore

PRACTICING BALANCE:

- *Be on the lookout for moments of imbalance.* Ask yourself if there may be an opposite missing or something present in excess that may be causing your singing problem. Think of Goldilocks or yin and yang. For example, in working hard to find the right sound are you trying *too* hard, using too much superfluous energy, or tension from the wrong place? Are you overly concerned with pleasing your teacher and focused on gaining approval? Or are you trying to be the singer you *think* your listeners want you to be, and in so doing, losing your ability to hear your Adviser? In looking for a beautiful sound all the time are you sacrificing emotional expression that may require something less than lovely to be effective? Remember that *"There is no energy unless there is a tension of opposites."*

- *Look out for and observe the ego in the singing process.* If you find yourself upset or frustrated with things happening in your singing, try to step back, and ask yourself what you need to do to make progress toward solving your problem. (This can apply to your career path, as well as to your technical or musical difficulties.) Make a list of what you want to achieve and the practical steps needed to achieve it. (Be aware that your emotional responses will not help here, so don't let them get in the way.) With your list in hand, simply move toward taking the next step; be honest about applying it and give up your excuses and simply stay on your path. View your ego as something outside of you that you are in control of not an inner power that controls you.

- *Begin to recognize the times when left- or right-brain function is dominant.* Then work to manage the switch from one to the other. For instance, if you have worked and worked on a piece to try to fix a couple of trouble spots, allow yourself to let go of trying to fix the details and go to the bigger picture. From a technical point of view, you may ask yourself:

  - Is my breath working?
  - Is my body fully committed?
  - Are the words clear?
  - Am I grounded and centered?

Or, from an emotional point of view:

  - What am I trying to convey?
  - How do I feel about the song as a whole?

Singing with focus on just one larger aspect can sometimes have the effect of fixing the details that are going wrong.

- *Practice emotional commitment, as well as technique in the studio.* Otherwise you may be caught off balance in performance.

- *Observe your responses in voice lessons.* Determine not to go to extremes just to try to please your teacher; be aware of fears as they surface and do your best not to be driven by them. Nurture an approach to learning that is just right— stay present, attentive, and take risks. The studio is, after all, a very safe environment. Open your mind and body to new experiences and maintain equanimity.

- *Nurture empathy between you and your audience.* When you have a concert or recital performance, walk on stage, and give yourself an opportunity to connect with your listeners. Make eye contact, smile, and take time to be *wholly present* with the people who have come to listen to you. Take a few deep breaths and put any fear of them or their judgment behind you. See them as the supporters they are. (Remember this is also true of the audition panel.) Alleviate your fear of them by imagining that the audience is the initiator of the conversation and that your song is an empathic response to a question or something expressed as concern by them. As you begin to sing, focus on the music, the words, your emotional connection to the song, and the *Gift* you are giving your audience but stay open to receiving the reciprocal energy they have to offer. In other words, even as you sing, keep "listening" to them. Be aware that it is not a one-way street. Feeling this flow of give and take can transform your experience of performing.

In every aspect of your singing, always seek balance.

A FINAL WORD

"It is not because things are so difficult that we do not dare;
it is because we do not dare that things are so difficult."
— Seneca

BACK ON YOUR JOURNEY

My suggestions are intended to illuminate your singing journey and lead you to a place where you can feel comfortable being the singer you have always wanted to be. I hope you have come to understand that, though you can expect it to be thrilling and enlightening, you cannot necessarily expect your journey to be easy. To sing well takes work, commitment, focus, and courage.

Before you can truly bring about the changes you need to make, you must ask yourself if it is possible that you are so attached to your bad habits and the way you sing now that you love them more than you love the idea of improvement? Singing better is a choice, and you must consciously choose the path toward the singer you want to be. The singer you *don't* want to be (the one you are now who is obviously not satisfied, otherwise you wouldn't be reading this book) cannot stay with you on the path.

Perhaps what I or your voice teacher are asking you to do to improve your singing is still very scary because in making the necessary changes, you may lose something before you even know what you will gain from the loss or what will replace it. As I said in the introduction, fear is an inhibiting factor in almost every aspect of our singing progress. Clearing the hurdle of fears is the biggest leap we can take.

So, along with working on some of the practices I've given you here, remind yourself whenever fear raises its head that it is essentially ego driven. The ego fears failure, responsibility, looking foolish, and being judged imperfect; the ego is the Controller

161

and the Judge who erect signs on our path declaring Be Afraid! But you do not have to allow the ego to remain in control. We have an alternative self—the Adviser, the Authentic Singer. The way to lessen the grip of our fears, then, is to deny the ego and strengthen that authentic voice, staying true to our intention to share our Gift, give to others, develop compassion toward our listeners, and tell our story with honesty while demanding nothing in return.

Courage is, after all, not a lack of fear. It is acknowledging fear and doing something anyway.

If we can turn our fears around, push them behind us (along with our Diva and our Introvert), what is revealed on the opposite side is awareness. Stay aware, experiencing each moment undistracted, and you will watch fear dissipate. It seems evident to me that fear does not exist if we stay in the present moment. Fear is rooted in the past (bad experiences) and the future (anticipation of what might happen). If you can keep sharpening your focus on what is happening as you sing, accept each moment for what it is as it happens, and avoid dwelling on what was or what might be, you will slowly find that fear becomes just a shadow in the background. You live in awareness.

This is what I call *objective presence,* the awareness of the Adviser. The Controller *belongs* to the world of fears and can't help you get to the other side of them. Through objective presence you stand back and observe each moment, alert and ready to address things that arise.

Of course, this is only the catalyst for your next exciting step. Once you become fully aware, it is up to you to make the choice to change. Awareness is the beginning, change is the path.

STILL ON MY JOURNEY

As for me, it took a very long time to learn all these things and to understand why I had such problems and obstacles on my singing path. It might seem I learned the lessons too late since you don't hear me singing at Covent Garden Opera House or Carnegie Hall, as I dreamed of in my youth. But the lessons I learned changed my dreams or at least made them clearer.

I discovered that all I really wanted was to be able to sing freely and authentically and share my songs with my audience. So whether I sing in an important concert or in an opera or to the senior citizens in a nursing home or at a wedding or in a school or to my friends or students, if I see one sparkle in the corner of an eye that says my listener is sharing something special with me and that I have made a difference if only for a moment in someone's life through my singing, then I know I have become the singer I want to be.

At this point in my life, I am now dealing with changes in my body and health issues due to aging; this is a new and daunting challenge that feels inevitable and uncontrollable. I am sometimes comforted to hear some of the great opera stars I aspired to emulate in my youth obviously struggling with some of the same problems in current recordings. I remind myself that a great performance is not about perfection but about commitment, not about making the most beautiful sounds but of singing with honesty, not about feeding my own ego but about enriching the lives of others.

Your Traveling Companion—the Song

I was recently on vacation in the Caribbean, dining in a beach café, and a Latin band was playing. The lead singer was a beautiful young woman with a powerful, authentic, captivating voice. She began a familiar, popular song and all attention was on her— she was in the spotlight, the adored diva. But as the song went on a few listeners stood up to dance and, because some were very good, focus shifted to them. After a few moments, the rest of the audience took their lead and began dancing or singing along with the chorus; everyone was now a performer of sorts and our attention now turned on ourselves. It was a thrilling and fun experience for us all, led by the band and the beautiful singer, but not all about them. The singer had imperceptibly faded into the background, and the song and the music had taken over. Everyone became active participants in an experience that united us all. The success of the singer was that she had handed us her Gift, selflessly, generously, and with full commitment to the music she was singing.

So even though *who you are* is the *very* heart of your singing, remember that surrounding you like a cocoon when you sing with honesty is the *song.* When the Authentic Singer sings, the song itself takes center stage; this is the humility of a great singer. If the song is filtered through the Diva or the Introvert, it is distorted by the ego. In effect, a glaring light is shone on us that reveals and even magnifies all our faults and flaws and makes the resulting judgment from our listeners all the more inevitable, all the more harsh and all the more difficult to separate from our sense of self-worth. Thus, exactly what we fear in the first place comes to pass! By singing authentically, we avoid throwing the spotlight on our less-than-perfect selves. Instead, *we become the song.*

FINALLY...STEPPING OUT

Applying all the practices I've suggested in this book will help you free your voice to be able to express yourself honestly through your singing. I will remind you once again, though, that this is not a substitute for vocal technique, which should be applied in parallel, complementing your knowledge of your physical instrument and how it works. But I know from experience that a voice teacher cannot always put you in touch with all the parts of yourself you need to be the singer you want to be. Nor can she connect all those parts into the whole. Only you can do that. It's my hope that this book has illuminated the path to the *heart* of singing for you. Working from that place to connect it all together is now up to you.

It is not necessary to have everything completely under your control to be able to sing. We all have moments of flagging energy when, for reasons we may not completely understand, we feel disconnected from ourselves, from our breath, from our emotions, and from our imaginations, and our bodies and minds just give up on some of the work. In those moments the voice will not work as well as we would like.

But try to accept that those moments are "just the way it is today," not your fault, not a result of your incompetence, and not moments to take away your worth as a singer or as a human being. In fact, they make you more fully human. Live with those moments and recognize them as part of the variables of the singer's life, part of our wonderful experience. Accept that if you always do your best with the way you are today and keep singing with authenticity—weary but still committed—you are on your way to being a great singer.

On your good days, when you can put into practice what we have discussed here and allow your authentic voice to sing to the world, you will free yourself to offer the gift of who you *are* and what you *feel* through the song you sing. You will act as a mirror and guide for other people to see themselves more clearly and look at the world with new eyes. Then you will watch in wonder as you are transformed into the singer you have always wanted to be.

Step out on your path.

Enjoy the journey.

Copy this list and keep it with you to remind yourself of your singing path:

- Sing what you love
- Present yourself to the world as a singer
- Focus on the song
- Be patient
- Commit yourself fully
- Understand the power of the mind
- Stay conscious—stay present
- Return to the breath
- Be aware of your whole body—keep it strong
- Be generous with your Gift
- Be honest with yourself and your audience
- Trust your inner voice—the Adviser
- Silence the Judge—learn to discern
- Take the risks
- Stop making excuses
- Take responsibility—don't blame others
- Remind yourself that perfection is an illusion
- Change your routine
- Invite the audience into your performance
- Don't try too hard
- Always do your best
- Be easy on yourself
- Take joy in every small step

BIBLIOGRAPHY

Campbell, Don G. *The Roar of Silence*. Wheaton, IL: Quest Books, 1989.

Csikszentmihaly, Mihaly. *Flow: The Psychology of Optimal Experience*. New York: Harper Perennial, 1991.

Dickinson, Emily. *Collected Poems*. Philadelphia: Courage Books, an imprint of Running Press Publishers, 1991.

Gass, Robert. *Chanting: Discovering Spirit in Sound*. New York: Broadway Books, 1999.

Hemsley, Thomas. *Singing and Imagination: A Human Approach to a Great Musical Tradition*. Oxford: Oxford University Press, 1998.

Jourdain, Robert. *Music, The Brain and Ecstasy*. New York: William Morrow and Company, Inc., 1997.

Kall, Robert. *Rob Kall*. http://www.robkall.com (accessed 2009 29-July).

Keyes, Laurel Elizabeth. *Toning: The Creative Power of the Voice*. Los Angeles: DeVorss and Co., 1973.

Kreutz, Gunter. "Effects of Choir Singing or Listening on Secretory Immunoglobin A, Cortisol and Emotional State." *Journal of Behavioral Medicine*, December 2004: 623-635.

Lawrence, D.H. *Complete Poems*. New York: Penguin Classics, 1994.

Lerner, Alan Jay and Loewe, Frederick. "Camelot." Los Angeles: Alfred Publishers, 1960.

Merton, Thomas. *Thomas Merton: Spiritual Master*. Edited by Lawrence S. Cunningham. Mahwah, NJ: Paulist Press, Inc, 1992.

Nelson, Samuel H. and Blades-Zeller, Elizabeth. *Singing with Your Whole Self: The Feldenkrais Method and Voice*. Lanham, MD: Scarecrow Press, Inc., 2002.

Newham, Paul. *Using Voice and Movement in Therapy*. London: Athenaeum Press, 1999.

Oliveros, Pauline. *Roots of the Moment*. New York: Drogue Press, 1998.

Rodenburg, Patsy. *The Right to Speak.* New York: Routledge, Inc., 1992.

Sassoon, Siegfried. *"Everyone Sang", from Collected Poems of Siegfried Sassoon.* New York: Viking Penguin, a division of Penguin Group (USA) Inc., 1918.

Spolin, Viola. *Improvisation for the Theater.* 3rd Edition. Evanston, IL: Northwestern University Press, 1999.

Suzuki, Daisetz T. In *Zen in the Art of Archery,* by Eugen Herrigel. New York: Vintage Books, 1953.

Taylor, Jill Bolte. *My Stroke of Insight: A Brain Scientist's Personal Journey.* New York: Plume, 2006.

Williamson, Marianne. *A Return to Love: Reflections on the Principles of a Course in Miracles.* New York: Harper Collins, 1992.

Zander, Rosamund Stone and Ben. *The Art of Possibility.* New York: Penguin Books, 2000.